Sand
in
My
Shoes

Bob Barsanti

ISBN: **978-0-6152-1131-2**
Copyright 2008 Bob Barsanti. All Rights Reserved.
Please send all correspondence to
Box 3289, Nantucket MA 02554

Or on the web at http://www.barrsenglishclass.com

Table of Contents

1. Introduction 1
2. Peepers 7
3. A Very Daffy Place 14
4. Hiring With Nantucket in Mind 20
5. Spring Creeps In 26
6. Memorial Day 32
7. The Ghosts That Walk Beside Us. 37
8. Wing to Wing and Oar to Oar 43
9. Our Best Work 49
10. The Well Kept Hedge 55
11. Independence Day 60
12. The Toypedo 66
13. I Love to Beat You 71

14. Drinking Champagne Every Day 76

15. A Cocoon of Fog..81

16. Why Did We Ever Come Here? 86

17. The Luxury of August................................92

18. Enduring..98

19. Let August be August 104

20. Cobbletones..110

21. Bricks in the Basement..............................115

22. The End of Something 122

23. Labor Day 128

24. September Song..134

25. Waiting for the Hurricane........................139

26. A Lover's Quarrel.......................................144

27. The Spiderweb that Connects Us.............150

28. The Moment of the Race Car Tent...........156

My enduring thanks go to

    Suzanne and Jerry Daub for continuing to publish me,

    Elizabeth Scanlon for her skills in editing,

    Sydney Fee Barsanti for her patience,

    Father James O'Rourke for his encouragement,

    And Rourke and Beck Barsanti for perspective.

1: Introduction

The island has been good to me. I will miss it.

I came to the island in 1987. I had graduated from college that spring and had spent the summer fruitlessly painting houses in Ipswich for an utterly clueless trust fund baby. His paychecks were random, my boredom was intense, and my adult life spread before me like one long bus ride. On a whim and friendly memory, I faxed a copy of my resume to John Sullivan, the principal of Nantucket High School and went on trudging through a hot summer of scraping and spilling. One call led to a visit and an interview, the next call led to a more serious talk with Dr. O'Neill and a ride back to town in his station wagon, wherein he offered me the job.

My first year on island was tough. I didn't own a car, so I biked back and forth to the old high school. Cable had just arrived on island, so I was able to watch Larry Bird occasionally, while my housemate kept himself amused watching MTV and filling the room with white smoke. I taught over 100 students in a building that had been condemned for a paycheck that barely covered rent and electricity. It was a hard year.

Many of the teachers I started with that September left that June. I understood full well why. I had also burnished my resume, culled some letters of recommendation, and cast a longing and loving eye to other schools. I was particularly interested in schools near ski areas. But, I worked through the summer and came back that September. And that became a habit. Returning to Nantucket seemed like a reasonable choice until it stopped actually being a choice. One winter afternoon, in the teachers' room, a friendly math teacher asked if this was the year that I would finally move on. At which point, Ritch Leone raised his head up and said that I wasn't going anywhere, I had "sand in my shoes."

I suppose I do. After twenty years, it's ground deep into the soles of my sneakers and my Bean boots, as well as into the floor of my car, in the bottom of all of my bags, and in the spines of my books. The sand anchors me to a place where I no longer live. Time and tide have conspired to nudge me off the island and place me in a town where the snow stays on the ground for months at a time. Gas, milk, Oreos, and three bedrooms/two baths cost a great deal less than they do on island. I can take classes, I can go to birthday parties, I can see the Red Sox on a Tuesday night. But, I still look out the window for the beach grass and scrub pines of Nantucket. When I walk out the door in the morning, I listen for the roar of the surf. The sand in my shoes are not anchors I have left on Nantucket, but anchors Nantucket has left in me.

I think there are two sorts of people that move away from Nantucket: those that return and those that don't. Those that don't return must have a gene that didn't dive into my pool; they must be able to put the memories in a box and close the closet. I throw the pennies from the boat, keep some Cisco sand on my desk, and cherish my Reds like an old letter sweater. Sentimentality haunts my every move.

Leaving Nantucket meant leaving all of its natural charms. I could list a hundred things that I miss, but the list would be incomplete. Nantucket gives you tiny gifts every moment. When you leave, you miss all the smallest of things that happen in the corner of your eye. You don't notice how dark the night sky is until the halogen turns it orange.

When I think of Nantucket at its best, I think of Sconset Golf Course. If you haven't played at Skinner's, you have missed a singular Nantucket experience. It's an awful course that seems to have been laid out a century ago by a frustrated farmer. The greens are thick with grass, and, by mid-summer, the fairways have burnt to a pale and dusty tan. The holes are short and the greens fees are expensive. Each year brings the threat that the Nantucket Golf Club will swallow it up and spit it back out as a driving range, parking lot, and skeet shooting platform. Or that the owner will pave the first hole and build a sub-division. In short, the course is everything that present Nantucket is.

Playing golf at Skinner's was never about the golf; any scorecard was suspect anyway. Instead, the course always showed you something. A huge hawk circled the second fairway. Swallows buzzed around the barn on the ninth like so many flies. Frogs and turtles pop up out of the water hazards. I loved walking the fairways in the late afternoon, setting a cold beverage on the grass, mis-hitting an iron, then picking up and moving on. I played alone, but the course also had the phone workers, the D.P.W., a renegade bartender and a few famous millionaires slumming with their bags on their shoulders. We waved at each other with easy distance of men; God forbid we should actually speak to each other.

More than the golf or those hundred little things, I miss the community. My old and dear friends remain old and dear friends; neither time nor distance can change that. But Nantucket is built by a thousand nods, waves, and smiles to people I only just recognize. A walk up Main Street or through the supermarket is interrupted by hundreds of brief exchanges. In contrast, my shopping at Big Y is done in silence.

In the end, that is what makes Nantucket different. We gossip at the strawberries, wave as we cross the milk section, and catch up with acquaintances in line. John

O'Neill still sees me in the frozen foods, two decades after giving me a ride to the boat. Ritch Leone stops me by the deli case. My old housemate avoids me in the cookie aisle. If we need quiet at the supermarket, we shop at night. And, even then, we find ourselves surrounded by friends and acquaintances who also want to be alone. We wave anyway.

I will return, the sand in my shoes will need to be replenished. I will tour the island as if I were in a Reunion class. Each stop on the tour will bring back a fond memory and a dark frown at the changes time and money has wrought over the winter. Then I will breathe deep and hold fast, looking, listening, and gathering all the little things that I hadn't missed until I left. Then, when it is time for me to leave again, I will scrunch my toes into the sand and wave.

2: Peepers

I am waiting for the peepers.

In our backyard, a small wetlands fills with the loud little amphibians once spring has started. As soon as they get the first few warm nights, the frogs will start peeping to one another. One little peeper makes the toot of a child's whistle. A thousand of them drown out the Cape Air planes.

For all of their noise, I don't know anyone who loathes them. I don't think Marine Home Center carries "peeper poison" or anti-peeper signs. Noone I know, other than one biology teacher, rounds them up for experiments. If they disturb sleep, noone complains of it.

It may be that, for all of their noise, we like the peepers. After the Melvillian silence of the winter, the adolescent roars of frogs in love gets our hope out of the closet. Like a Red Sox cap, hope looks good in spring.

On the way out, winter drags its feet. It dawdles over coffee, cracks its knuckles, and checks the addition. The ice still hides in the shadows of the walls and in the high grass. The wind is cold enough to keep most of the kids off the playgrounds. The D.P.W.'s sand fills the streets and parking lots.

Back in September, I couldn't wait for winter to visit. Winter held so much promise to me when I was stuck in traffic. Stuck on Sparks Avenue behind the Escalades and the Hummers, I wanted the cold winds to blow them all back to Connecticut and Hobe Sound. As Caliban was charged, I wanted it to clear the island of its invaders and restore it to its "rightful" owners. In my ideal winter, I could walk Main Street and see only familiar faces, read the books that had been accreting on my bedroom table, and watch those storms blow in.

When winter did come, it snuck on-island sometime after Halloween and spent the next four months lurking. During some years, we get a winter from Canada. The storms come spiraling up from Hatteras, the cold air locks in over us and the snow swirls and drifts over harbor ice. This year, the only snow came on the calendar.

Snow is winter's champagne; we all splurge and get a little silly in it. Buildings, trash, hedges and all are drunkenly transformed by the snow so the island becomes a party. Cemeteries become playgrounds, streets become ski hills, and the storm becomes a story. This winter, there was no party. Our bad acts hung in front of us like blown trash in the blackberry bushes.

Winter on Nantucket rests in browns and grays. The elms, the scrub oaks, the blackberries are skeletal gray. They clatter together in the wind. Beneath them, the grass blows tan and hushed. The harbor freezes and night, then melts in the day. Out at the beaches, the clouds turn purple in mid-afternoon and the great clouds of ocean ducks line the horizon. We measure the hours in darkness and scars.

So much of an island winter disappoints. Winters fireworks have been few and far between. Teeth chattering, shingle tearing, legendary nor'easters threaten every fortnight of so, then either whirl majestically far out to sea and give the fish snow days or dive inland and drench children's dreams in forty-five degree rain and wind. The ice hasn't been firm enough to allow for pond hockey or even a few wobbly steps. It has been a winter of mud, drizzle, and silence.

Business has disappointed as well. As realty has slowed, so has the client dinner and the "Get to Know You" lunch. I sat downtown at a bar for a burger the other day, and talked politics with three realtors for an hour or so. The chef, with his New Orleans specials simmering on the stove, appeared every few minutes to appraise the empty room and to upbraid the bartender for not pushing the jambalaya. This restaurant had hoped for a decent winter. Several others had given up, closed the doors, and hunkered down until their workers and their customers returned in the spring.

Hopefully.

Doubt grows faster than the bills in January and February. The long-running billion-dollar banquet of island real estate may be down to a few soft pieces of celery, a cold meatball, and some lonely slices of goose liver pate. For weeks, the Land Bank has racked up little money in transfer fees, because nothing was transferring. The realtors play Minesweeper and the lawyers make vacation plans. The air of Cliff Road and Tom Nevers has been notably silent. You can hear the belts tightening.

Hope can be a curse. One bad summer became two, which begat three, four, and five. Pretty soon, even the dimmest can pick up a pattern. The new commercial lease arrives in February, then hope and doubt both sit at the table, looking through the fine print. Hope carries the advantage of habit and history: doubt holds the numbers. You wish in one hand, you spit in the other. Meanwhile, the roof leaks in heavy rain, the kids aren't doing so well in school, and your neighbor just moved to Lenox. When do you stop hoping?

Now, I hope for a good spring. The crocuses have started to poke up in the Denby Real Estate garden. Six meadowlarks have been spotted looking for a summer rental close to town. The osprey have returned to the water views, the oyster catchers scout for restaurants and the cormorants hunt for a mooring. Daisuke and his amazing gyroball will be appearing regularly at Fenway. The Flying Hammer Squads are back on the roofs and walls of the town. The potholes and ponds of Nantucket roads grow larger and larger.

But, still no peepers.

I have confidence that they will be here with the daffodils and the antique cars. Like Ariel, they will call the sailors to the shore. Already, the first seasonal residents have slipped back onto the island and are making plans to re-open the restaurants, inns, and shops of the summer. The help-wanted ads have doubled and tripled in the last few weeks as landscapers and innkeepers get ready for the summer onslaught. The Stop and Shop has more and more unfamiliar faces, from Connecticut, Guatemala and Jamaica.

Their buzz is mostly unintelligible to this Anglo, but welcome nonetheless.

In spring, I look forward to seeing and hearing from all of seasonal residents again, whether they be migrant lawnmowers, plutocrat golfers, or peepers. They see the island as a fresh and brave new world of waves and seagrass and ocean breezes. In their eyes, the dull landscape I have been imprisoned in, brightens. The island, to them, is a place of relaxation, redefinition, and riches. After a winter of mini-malls and inter-office memos, they come out here to the dream of Nantucket. And greet it with a lusty peep.

3: A Very Daffy Place

I left my cynicism and wallet at home and went with the crowd at Daffy Day this year. It was a very Nantucket Daffy Day; the predicted horrible weather held off and the island was bright, almost green and the daffodils, for once, were blooming on cue. Moreover, the cars and the crowd held more familiar faces than I remembered. Hammie and the Thundering Heard were nervously waiting for backfire; Bill Haddon and Manny Dias were showing off their decorating abilities, while the rest of the parade featured VW microbuses, a Corvette, and a few trucks.

On the way out to Sconset, the Island Homers, as well as a few dozen other well-wishers waited just past the rotary. They came with folding chairs, lunches and napkins. The old guard of Natives was also out, bestowing a blessing on the cars. Due to the weather forecast, Daffy Day lost its Travel Channel allure for the Gulfstream guys and gals but brought back the islanders. The volume of natives in the parade and along the route cheered my heart. If we can reclaim Daffy Day for the islanders, perhaps we could get the Christmas Stroll back as well?

Unfortunately, the one discordant note to the whole proceeding came on the way to Sconset. We were looking for large plywood cutouts of animals. Each year they were different. They could be elephants, lions, giraffes or even a Thompson's gazelle or an Udu. However, the animals of the Serengeti didn't make the migration this year. The moors were just the moors; beautiful and handsome, but not particularly Daffy.

Nantucket can be a very Daffy place. Our oddballs and eccentrics don't get stuffed into closets as they do in America; they get elected to important boards and wear the mantles of authority. As a result, barely a season goes by without a hokey ceremony or tradition. In the winter, Curtis Barnes walks around ringing a bell and we have a spelling bee. In the spring, we celebrate a broken down firetruck and have an Iron Man, the Fourth of July has another fire truck skirmish on Main Street while the fall features a parade of ghosts and Power Rangers followed by a icy dip in the harbor.

I think these events are charming and not greedy. Greedy events exist only for the taking of money. If you removed the money, the event would disappear. I think we would still have Stroll if none of the tourists showed. Main Street would be filled with old cars if there wasn't a dime to be made. Our history is filled with odd, hokey events that no longer grace the calendar but show how eccentric you can become living out here in the sea. Sheep shearing festivals, corn husking festivals, the Madaquecham Jam, Pirate Day, the Mad Hat Luncheon, the P.T.A. day, and the Redman's Parade have all marched into the libraries and archives but are remembered fondly.

Our love of the odd and eccentric comes from two facets of our island. First, we are a small town out in the sea. Small towns, for all their conformity and peer-pressure, insulate and support oddballs. The math teacher may only wear purple, but she is a pretty good math teacher, so we set the purple sweaters to the side. The selectman may talk to himself and read poetry at the selectman's meetings, but he seems to know what he is talking about.

Second, the governing ethos of the island has been Wharf Rat Democrat: "No seat is reserved for the mighty." The mighty didn't control much on the island so there was no need to look for their approval or fear their disapproval. Since the demise of the Quaker faith, there are no binders or protocols to codify everyone's appropriate behavior. A math teacher who only wore purple may make others uneasy and may violate the dress code. A quiet word, a note in a file, and she wears the same shade of beige as her Toyota. Closing Main Street for a water fight would upset business, cause a traffic jam, and invoke huge overtime for the police. America would never stand for it.

Daffy Day is a product of the Wharf Rat Democrat. Everyone can be a part of the Daffiness for the weekend. It's important to acknowledge that the pleasures of Stroll, Daffy Day and the like come to those people who either own a house here or who can afford to come. However, noone needs a ticket to go out to see the cars. The Model T's and

Studebakers don't pull into the "Members only" lot for special private viewing by the Friends of the Daffodil. Car owners and sponsors don't have a special, catered dinner prepared for them. Everyone can make a funny hat with the flowers. The only restriction remains on getting in the parade. You need an old car and a check. Since they are letting in VW Beetles these days, the bar seems to be dropping.

The Wharf Rat Democrat has been good to Nantucket; these events have become lucrative. They bring the visitors from the American Mall. Once they are on the sand, they are welcome to wear yellow and walk up Main Street. Lawyer and landscaper, baker and banker, cook and crook can all dress like bananas and wander among the Model A's, Camaro's, and trucks. We sell them all lunch, dinner, put them up for the night, and send them back with a calendar and a fifteen dollar t-shirt.

I suspect that whoever made the animals of the Serengeti was a Wharf Rat Democrat. I prefer to believe a long-standing island shop and builder made them on the sly and propped them up with the winking of various officials. With their sudden absence this year, I fear that Del Wynn was the springtime zoo-keeper. And Del, unfortunately, is no long with us.

I hope that the Wharf Rat Democrat finds a way to remain. The island is no longer a friendly place for him. Instead, we are creating more and more seats for the mighty. More private golf clubs, sailing clubs, and tennis clubs chop up the island. Passkeys, Gate attendants, and parking stickers separate the mighty from the many. Any non-profit on this island has more patron's circles than Dante's inferno. While we need the money for the various causes, we have to know what we are selling. And it isn't just a seat in the sand.

Eventually, the older Wharf Rat Democrats will move on to either the Bosom of Our Lord or Naples, Florida. The next generation needs to look, carefully, at what they are willing to sell. As my mother-in-law said, what you don't own, you don't control. The fewer seats we reserve for the mighty, the better our island will be for all of us. It will remain a haven for the odd and eccentric, with their bow ties and fire engines, only if we act to keep it that way. Otherwise, we may never see the animals of the Serengeti again.

4: Hiring with Nantucket in Mind

You can't see Nantucket from the mainland. Unlike the Vineyard, it doesn't hang right off shore so close that a sunfish or a particularly energetic swimmer could dream of paddling over for lunch before heading back with the tide. From Falmouth, you can see the lights in the summer, the houses along East Chop, and the traffic backing up on State Road in Oak Bluffs.

Even from Chatham, Nantucket only is visible in the imagination or memory or some combination of the two. Mainlanders remember what it was like when they last visited the Old Mill and Henry's, but their memories radiate with age. If they never crossed the sound, they might imagine a place where Kerry, Lamar, and Jack Welch wear their swimsuits and wait in line at the market for kippered herring in cream.

To those Americans, the island becomes an imaginary place, where the normal social rules of silence, averted glances, and isolation have been chucked into the dumpster. Instead, our Neverland runs on first names, compassion and pixie dust. We believe it. Out here, Nantucket's "specialness" has become faith and dogma. We want the island to be a better place where neighbors can talk to neighbors, preferably before they take a bulldozer to all of the blueberry and blackberry bushes on their property.

All weekend, I saw folks who had drunk the Kool-Aid. The Clean Team was walking the Madaket Bike Path. They picked up old trash bags, empty cans, and the occasional thesis paper hidden in the beach plums and bamboo. At Tom Nevers' Playground, a diaper bag sat at the top of a picnic table, waiting for the forgetful father to come back and pick it up. Near Mitchell's, I saw a set of keys on the bench, placed smack dab in the middle where all eyes were attracted to it. We must live in an exceptional place, where a set of car keys would sit out in plain sight, waiting for the rightful owner to pick them up. So many things make Nantucket exceptional, from the beaches to the moors to the Chief waving on the road; those patient and waiting keys are its most remarkable feature.

Natives are not the only true believers. Our recent summer arrivals, the membership of Nantucket Golf Club, Westmoor, and Great Harbor Yacht Club are on the same page. They put on fundraising and charitable events throughout the summer including a golf tournament that raises enough money to fund most of the pre-schools on island and to send two graduates to college on a free ride. Rich and poor, young and old, we cross the water to live in the world that we would like to see. I want to live in a place where doors don't need locks, phones are answered by people, and you drive with one hand while waving with the other.

And I am willing to pay for that dream. I am willing to pay exorbitant prices not only to get things shipped here, but to employ my friends. I am willing to sacrifice the comfortable mask of anonymity. I am willing to patiently endure the angry parent because he will still come at 9:00 on Friday night to restart my furnace. I see all of those sacrifices as worth it, not because I want to live in a place where the surf report is important. I want to live in a place where everybody knows your name.

After a few years, those who hire on island seem to forget about the sacrifices necessary in order to become one of the Lost Boys. At this point, whenever I read in the I&M about a "nationwide search," I know that it will finish in a disaster, either for the town or the newbie. Too many of our "managers" think that they were hired to solve a problem. In order to solve the problem, they figure they should avoid the on-island rubes and know-nothings, and hire someone with real qualifications. The newbie comes ashore with his resume, recommendations, and good ideas then runs into the dream of Nantucket and all of the costs of that dream. Then she leaves. You have to pay a lot more than money to work out here.

First, you have to work all the time. Off-island, you can be a doctor with regular hours and rounds. The patients visit Monday through Friday, with a half day on Wednesday for golf. Out here, your patients will call you at home and roust you for a prescription. They will line up at the back door at the end of office hours for a quick word. Since these folks aren't just patients, they are your daughter's music teacher, your wife's best friend, or the guy who was supposed to come to fix the leak in the roof. Every relationship is a personal one, none are professional.

Second, you are on a stage as soon as you walk out of your house. Friends, enemies and strangers will wave to you from your car and will wonder why you are wearing jeans. You can't get blotto at the Box and become invisible. Instead, you will become the pearl of rumor and legend. Early in my teaching career, I worked as a bouncer. On a slow Thursday night, I graded vocabulary quizzes on the back bar accompanied by three pie-eyed ladies. On Friday morning, I learned that all three were mothers of students who complained to the principal about my grading papers at a bar. Someone is always watching.

Third, money will be tight. Even if you are a realtor selling acres of air conditioning or the star plumber of the catwalk, the money will not come in as regular as the bills will. Nor will you have time to do all of the billing and paperwork that you need to. And, even when the money sprays in a torrent, around the corner of the calendar comes the storm, or the collapse, or the fire that will take it all away.

Finally, you will need to forgive. The Yates gas guys will have to go into a house and turn off the gas on a family. They could have small kids or they could have crack pipes on the window sills, but they will be on the island with you. Their son will play football with your son. Out here, you can have very few enemies. Enemies, once made, tend to play golf with your boss and write letters to the paper. At the least, they turn out to be the dental hygienist with the floss in her fingers.

Everyone who hires, be it principal or postal worker, should sit down and read "Hiring With Nantucket in Mind." The most qualified, the cheapest, or the most experienced aren't necessarily the first qualities you need in an employee. Rather, the employees need to believe. They need to believe so much in the dream of Nantucket that they will be willing to work 80 hours a week and see their family only in pictures. They need to give up closing doors and drawing shades. They need to fear the coming financial waterspout and they need to hold their tongue until it bleeds.

But, if they can do all that, they could leave their car keys on the park bench in the morning and pick them up in the afternoon.

5: Spring Creeps In

Spring comes to Nantucket in a slow, tardy creep. The wind stays cold, the puddles freeze overnight and the great, gray, over cast stays firmly pressed down on the horizon.

An island winter comes to its darkest, bleakest depth in March, after spring skiing and the Grapefruit League are in full swing. While the sailors on the Chesapeake burn their socks on the first day of spring, Nantucketers reach, again, for the polar fleece. Nantucket's winters aren't particularly harsh weather-wise. On the best of winters, we don't get much colder than Virginia or North Carolina. On the worst, we move to the coast of Maine or even New Brunswick. Snow melts before our one plow can get to it all and, even the coldest snap, ends in the forties.

No, the teeth of Nantucket's winter are dull, yellow, and flecked. The colors of summer drain away in a low burn during late October leaving the landscape brown, black, and gray. Then the sky mirrors those colors, the wind blows sand and salt everywhere, and we lock ourselves into the world of DVD's, Seagram's, and knitting.

After the houses on Monomoy, Squam, and Fair Street close up, our houses float in an inky sea, like the fishing boats moored off the south shore in the storms. From them, we dance a long, intricate dance with our neighbors. You drop off the kids at the same time as Judy, pick them up at the same time as John, go shopping at the same time that Jim does, and go out to dinner at the same restaurant, at the same time, with Jeff and Joan Johnson. Familiarity breeds with contempt under the blankets of civility.

By the time town meeting and town elections roll into early April, the quiet nasty words in the privacy of the front seat become the rolling mutter at the restaurant. The constant long-term nibbles of island living become shark bites. Each new basement is an insult, each zoning article is a theft, and each election becomes a tong war waged in bumper stickers, signs, and buttons. Nantucket may be the only town left in the United States where a Selectman's bumper sticker will cause frozen silences, sharp words, and hurt feelings.

Layer upon layer of grime builds up during the winter. The dump closes in on its legal limit, the sewer bills and estimates climb, the gas and heating oil prices spike, the bounced check notices roll in, and every familiar old view becomes the prize possession of a new picture window. And, just as we are about to list the house on the market and we will go under for the third time, Spring makes a reservation.

In my backyard, the blackberry bushes fall into a Jurassic tangle of gray branches, blown trash, and thorns. They lie open to the sky like a crushed rib cage. And then, right around the election, the daffodils bloom in the direct center. Still cold, still gray, still raw, spring has placed a marker. Then, after a few warmer days into the fifties, the peepers start.

When I step outside into the dark to once again encounter the hand of God near the trashcans, the sounds of spring rise up from the reeds, swamps, and bushes. The birds have come, the peepers call out, and the great frozen hunter sets early in the west. If close my ears, its still winter. The wind whips, the cold and damp seeps in, and the silence hangs just over the roll of a distant waves. But it is the feel of morning, thirty minutes before the alarm goes off.

Amid the brown and black, the splashes of yellow push up and out into the daylight of our consciousness. It's time to fertilize the lawn. It's time to finish shingling the rectory. It's time to lay the new pipe. It's time to hire for the summer. It's time to make good on the thousands of decisions and indecisions that we pushed off in the during our electronic and alcoholic cocoon.

So, shortly after the daffodils, come the landscaping trucks and the "Opening Soon" signs; the light brown of new shingles and the thump of nail guns. On the mainland, temperatures have already touched 75 and the ski areas are melting like ice cream in the sun. Shirtless boys are throwing lacrosse balls and the girls bravely lay out on their blankets. Polarfleece and wool remain the order of the day, but our eyes look to the sky.

The correct scientific name for a Daffodil is Narcissus. Narcissus, as Ovid writes, was a remarkably handsome young man who wouldn't fall in love with Echo (or any other young lady). Instead of a young lady, he famously falls in love with his own reflection and remains locked by the side of a pool, staring at himself until, at last, he is transformed into a Daffodil.

Unlike Narcissus, Nantucketers spend most of the winter hating themselves and avoiding the mirror. Each time they look into it, they see new lines, new creases, and an extra chin that seems to have risen from your collar. Our handbasket gets several miles closer to hell every day. Plutocrats, Pollution, and Politics pock mark our face. Each newspaper brings out a new rash or boil.

With the coming of the daffodils, we bend over the waters and see ourselves face to face, and fall in love again. The first gold of nature gilds the tips of the branches and the furze of the moors. The great gift of spring time is that we can fall in love with the island again. The colors return, the flowers bloom, and we can sit by the water, enamored of what we see.

Our troubles have not melted. The dump remains intractable, as does the rising cost of everything, and the incredible pressure we put on our politicians to solve all of our problems while not taking any of our money. We need to remember that moving to Nantucket was, at one point, the consummation and commitment of love. Like a marriage, we fight and become disillusioned with our great gray spouse. But, also, we can feel the warm rush of love in the spring.

6: Memorial Day

I woke up this morning to the sounds of summer, but the chill of winter. Outside my window, the birds had been up and chattering, the southwest wind rattled the crabapple branches, and, in the distance the surf broke. Nantucket's greatest sound is silence; in between the birds and ocean, silence rests. To those of us lucky to live here month after month, year after year, the silence becomes as familiar as the community.

To our visitors, the silence announces itself. The cars aren't racing by, far off, on the interstate, a trash truck is not beeping in reverse a half mile away, the ordinary hum and hiss of compressors and engines buzz at the edge of your attention. On island, those noises rest underneath the silence. On Memorial Day, the first marker of summer, our visitors come to the island and soak the silence in.

They are soaking other things in as well. At the end of May, the island has gotten itself ready for the prom. The fairways are lush, the ice cream line is empty, the littlenecks are cold and plentiful and the bluefish have begun to bite. For islanders, Memorial Day is either the end of a quiet winter or the beginning of a prosperous summer. For our visitors, Memorial Day brings respite and relaxation. The noise, the smell, and the chaos of the mainland fades in the fog.

Being Memorial Day, you have to feel more than a tad guilty to be enjoying the island summer. We are a nation at war, after all. We have been at war in Iraq longer than we were at war in the Pacific. On the afternoon that we drink imported beer on the deck and watch the blue fog roll in, six more Americans who never heard of the word Madaquecham, will die in a horrific explosion. More will find their way to Ramstein Airforce Base in Germany for emergency medical procedures. Some will lose an eye but regain their lives.

As Americans, this war is fought on TV and in the privacy of other people's homes. We don't ration, we don't turn off our lights at night, we don't get taxed for it (yet), we don't make U.S.O. packages, we don't contribute to lint drives. At most, we pause on days like this one for a momentary wave of guilt. Our memorial is in the icebox, next to the cold cuts.

We have many war memorials on island, and, unfortunately, we are likely to have several more. For an island founded and built by pacifists, the island has a long and active history in American Wars. Island boys slipped out to warships during the revolution and the War of 1812. They signed up, en masse, for the Civil War and for World War II, then a brave few have served since in Vietnam and in the Middle East. A dozen or so Whaler graduates have served, and, probably will continue to serve, in the current war.

After the Civil War ended, the town put a memorial smack dab in the middle of Main Street. That war had exacted a heavy cost to the former farmers and whalers of the island. The builders of the memorial didn't want these names fading into a field. Instead, they placed it in the dead center of town (in those days) with a grindstone at its base.

They wanted that war to be unavoidable, even to the Escalades and F150's that come racing down Main Street.

Presumably, the town fathers of 1875 wanted the heroism of the dead remembered. Many of those who died, perished in combat with the ideals of the nation on their back. Many others died of dysentery and diarrhea; war deaths do not always make good stories. Too often, it is the "useless slaughter of gallant men."

Leander Alley was one of those gallant men. He had been the first mate of a whale ship before the whale ships had gone away. When George Nelson Macy had returned to the island in search of volunteers, he signed up and left for Boston as a private in the Army. As a first mate, he was at the right hand of God on a whaleship. As a private in the army, he was under God's heel. Yet, he thrived. After the "hurricane of bullets" at Ball's Bluff, he was promoted to First Sargeant. Then, at Fredericksburg, he died attacking the fortifications at Marye's Heights. His body was returned to the island at Christmas. The schools and businesses closed, the funeral was performed, and the first military burial occurred on Nantucket. Seventy-one more Nantucketers would die in that war. The memorial features the name Leander Alley, of course, as it does the rest of the men, whether they died on the march or by the cannon.

Some of our more civic-minded folks have proposed moving the memorial. It slows the traffic flow, confuses the tourists, and doesn't allow for up-close study, unless you happen to be pinned to the passenger seat and stuck behind a delivery truck. One wag would put it in the center of our new rotary, so that drivers would have to travel over more Belgian block in order to hit it.

Being a curmudgeon, I like the memorial right where it is. In the summer, when the fish are biting, the surf is up, and the dinner reservation is waiting, the obelisk slows us all down. In these days, when the war is only on pay cable and the internet, it reminds us not only of honor and sacrifice, but also the stupidity and savagery of war. Would that it could slow the nation down on the way to war the way that it slows us down on the way to the beach.

7: Ghosts Who Walk Beside Us

The ghost tours are back.

A few years ago, an enterprising young man figured out that a loud voice, a few stories, and some good walking shoes could be the keys to wealth. And he was right. Without employees, rent, insurance, overhead, or even day-time work, he lined up dozens of people every night to pay him twenty bucks, to walk the streets and hear ghost stories.

Now, I am skeptical of most ghost stories. A willing audience, an inadvertent light left on, and a quick bit of creative self-promotion can create the ghost of a widow looking to the sea. On other hand, I have spend enough time knocking about old houses on Nantucket to know a few odd happenings and visits that can't be explained by a twenty dollar bill. Indeed, I have come to believe firmly in the spirits of Nantucket, but noone tells their stories on night-time walks.

Every ghost story starts at the question "Why?" An old man dies alone in his house. Why should his spirit haunt the building that he was confined in? A young girl falls into a well. Why shouldn't she go to a better place rather than rattling the wheel? Perhaps, like Hamlet's ghost, we are meant to believe that they are "doomed for a certain time to walk the night." But what could the girl who fell down the well have done to leave her doomed and cursed?

As a result, most ghost stories are light on the ghost and heavy on the story. And the true stories of old Nantucket are horrific enough to ruin more than a few dinners. Imagine running into Captain Paddock, walking a night watch, and get waylaid by his story of cannibalism. The mill spun all night because a manic miller was in there grinding corn. Samuel Comstock and Isaac Hussey spilled more than enough blood to fill the streets. A ghost would just be the nail on which to hang a historically horrific scene.

But the spirits of Nantucket have no story. They are nails without bloody scenes. They don't leave cold mists, or open doors, or dancing footsteps. They leave buildings.

Richard Wilbur built the Old Mill. By every document we can find, he did it mostly on his own. He hewed the beams, lifted the stones, and shaped the wheel. The work of his hands 250 years ago stands the test of time and grinds corn to this day. His spirit, silent and watchful, stands on the third floor of the mill and watches his wheel spin.

The spirit of Frederick Brown Coleman haunts the Atheneum. Those columns, and the historic capitals, medallions, and moldings came from both his mind and his hands. Rebuilt right after the Great Fire, those columns have withstood one hundred and fifty years of fog, rain, snow, frost, and meddling do-gooders. He does not rattle the chains in the rare books selection, but sits at a table and looks out across the harbor.

Spirits walk around us, all day and all night. What they built has endured. They stand on the corner and point up at the roofline or the eaves and say, "I built that." Were we only to stop for a moment, we would see them and hear their call. Instead, we rush to the bank, the boat, and the liquor store, with the radio on and a cell phone in the ear.

We only listen after we have dropped a twenty. Then we can walk up the streets that we rush up otherwise and hear the tales, real or imagined, of the folks who nailed the wood together. If we don't drop the money, we don't think it is important. We are too annoyed at the newspaper, or at the latest employee to walk out, or at the surprise houseguests, to see how well the front windows catch the light or how well the house opens onto the street.

I have spent much of the last year trying to help young men look into their hearts and figure out how they can make a difference in the world. They are immersed in culture that tells them that touchdowns, dollar bills, and sexual adventures make you a man. Yet, at any moment, they can look up at a hand-hewn beam and say "This was built to last." That beam will last far longer than Fifty Cent.

If you stand in the East Room at the Oldest House, you stand upon wooden planks eighteen to twenty four inches across. Someone selected that tree for his house, cut it, shipped it to the island, and fit it into the floor. And the boards, the fireplace, the beams, have lasted three centuries of benign neglect and malevolent restoration. Whoever built the house made a difference. He made a difference for his family and for his community. We stand on his handiwork and say "This is the way it should be done. Like this." More lessons are laid in oak planks than are printed on sheets of paper.

When we ask young people to make a difference in their communities, we are not asking them to learn how to peg a house or hoist a beam. We are asking them to find their talents and invest them. We want them to not only build sewers and churches, but to write, to paint, to fish, to preach or to sweep streets. If they commit themselves to their talent, they will become spirits. They may not haunt their buildings, but they will haunt protected open space, a classroom, the town building, the museum, or the hospital. A man can build a house without wood or tools.

Perhaps it is because I have started seeing the salt enter the pepper of my hair, but I have been accompanied by spirits on island. I hear Charlie Flanagan's voice at the school and hear Mary Walker's step on the stairs. Bernie Grossman drums his fingers on the Selectman's table and Sandra Fee slices roast beef behind the counter. David Ozias is out on the waves and Paul Morris is on the pier. And, like John Henry, I hear Del Wynn's hammer "make that cold steel ring."

There are millions of other ghosts wandering the moors. They whisper in the wind and crouch on the beach and they are unremembered. We only remember the ones that changed the world. The sad, the violent, the morose and the lonely may make a good yarn to spin to tourists, but the real Nantucket spirits stand in the shadow of their achievements. Look for them there.

8: Wing to Wing and Oar to Oar

The rain falls on everyone's weddings these days. I was invited to a recent celebration that had been envisioned out on the cranberry bogs, with wide open sky and gentle rolling horizon. Instead, the rain faucets came wide open and we were swept back to the "Where O Where House" for a hastily, and tastefully, organized ceremony on the back deck. A hundred or so of us were jammed into the little white chairs, tucked into each other's armpits, while the bride and groom negotiated an aisle with two huge posts in it. Even though the ceremony went off well, it wasn't the vision of the perfect day the bride and the photographers must have had.

What wedding or marriage is that perfect vision? Ten years down the line, your spouse is much more likely to remember the gaps, missteps and stinky fingers of the day, then all of the flawless ceremony. Marriage, as Rocky said, is all about gaps: "I got gaps, you got gaps. We fill each other's gaps."

Nantucket weddings have their own peculiar gaps. Fog, wind, and wave interfere with the assembly. You can't get the right band, the right flowers, or the right food for the right price. However, if you don't expect too much, you will be surprised by the gifts you do receive. I have heard Ted Anderson opine about the symbolism of the ring fifteen times, yet it always reverberates in my mind and on my hand. Old friends from far away places drop in for the ceremony; they tell enough of the story of their lives so that you want to be with them again. Then, they are gone. Inevitably, a guest or two arrives who should have their entrails hanging from the Harbor House ceiling, yet you smile and shake his hand and ask after the Red Sox. For that moment, all of us who were separate are together again on the beach, watching the boat leave.

Weddings bring many new folks onto our beach; for a weekend, they are islanders. In addition to affection of the wedding, they are romanced by the island. Nantucket is the mother of every island bride; she shapes the event more than any caterer or wedding planner. The guests see the sperm whale's bones, feel the wind on the moors, eat a striped bass, stand barefoot on the beach and the Gray Lady pours another intoxicating draft. The wedding guests drink of the silence and the surf, the roses and the romance, the cobblestones and the cranberries and they go back home with a happy, giddy island buzz, a shot of amour and a salt water chaser.

Most weddings have very little to do with the happy couple and everything to do with the guests. The two declare their love and commitment in front of us, so that we can hold their feet to the fire when the going gets tough. But they go and spin out into their lives. For the guests, a wedding brings a reckoning, not only of the bill, but of lives. When we see the newlyweds, we see what will be or what was.

Weddings have three different sorts of guests. First, the most energetic guests are the ones who have never been married. They see themselves hopefully transposed onto the central figures, but with a more panache. These are the ones who judge the bridesmaid's gowns, take pictures of the cake, and remember if the band played "Daddy's Little Girl" or

"Paradise by the Dashboard Lights." They come to a wedding as shoppers; they try on outfits and practice styles. They also come to the wedding ready to party. To them, a wedding is a celebration of love, alcohol, and friendship. They are easy to find; they are all at the after-party.

    Second, most of the guests have already been married. In their bones, they remember the fun and joy of the wedding day, and all of the blood, sweat, toil, and tears that followed it. They also see themselves transposed onto the bride and groom, but they remember how it was for them. They may have been silly, drunk, in love, or amazed, but now, looking back, they knew they were naïve. Marriage is a lot like Nantucket. You come here in the spring or the summer, when the air is warm, the money is easy, and surf is up. Then, the wind changes, everyone leaves, your checks bounce, and the great grey lid comes down. Then it gets worse. Every couple has a dark night in January, when life on the mainland would be a lot easier. Success comes when you decide to stay and wait for June.

Finally, the most important guests won't arrive and won't be eating cake. These could be the unborn children that will come a few years downwind. They are unspoken guests in the minds of parents, grandparents, and the couple themselves. In the congregation, someone is not only bearing witness to the union, but doing the familial dihybrid cross. He is adding his height to her athleticism and hoping for a tight end who could actually catch the ball.

The dead are there as well. Aunts, Uncles, Grandfathers, Grandmothers loom in the background with smiles as the chain moves on through time. Their absence is present in most minds. Everyone takes a sorrowful attendance at weddings and mourn for the empty chairs against the wall. Inevitably, the party has its own members who will slip into that good night before the next wedding comes around. They may be sick, they may be aged, or they may be called off to fight a war in a desert.

The groom was almost the exact same age as Casey Sheehan. Life called him to other paths than Casey followed. On April 4, 2004, he was busily researching mosquitoes and funny diseases, and not receiving small arms fire and rocket propelled grenades in Baghdad. As a result, he lived to see his wedding day and Casey didn't. Perhaps Casey was there as a silent guest.

    The newlyweds float in the center of all of us. Carried on the stream of our good wishes, hopes, and love, they bounce from table to table as if they are riding a leaf in a stream, then spin in circles in the dance floor. As the summer passes and fall arrives, that stream will not so much dry up as "go underground." The love that springs from their lips and the hope that bangs a fork on a water glass will become the breakfast for two, the made bed, and quiet consideration of passionate friends, traveling through the years wing to wing, and oar to oar.

9: Our Best Work

Classrooms were not made for June; they were made for November. In the fall, the wind whips in off the North Atlantic and the kids run to the warmth and light of the school. From the window, they watch the scallopers motor out into the purple overcast and the white flecked harbor and they thank their lucky stars for literary terms and the FOIL method.

But in June...The students come in with shirts and shorts, hats and sunscreen. Homework disappears, books get paged through, and sweat soaks through the teacher's hair and into his collar. Out here, we can see the bikes pass, the jeeps wait in traffic, and the sailboats glide across the harbor. Bumblebees and birds dart in and then out of the classroom, and a thick yellow frosting of pollen drifts over the book.

The humidity builds and lines up inside the over their desks and under the fluorescent lights. We open all of the windows as far as they will, but the line never moves. Only when the secretaries violate the fire code and open the front doors, does the air finally begin running out the door.

And the wind follows the Seniors. They scribble their finals, pay their bills, go to the prom, and practice for graduation. On island, we send the kids on their way with a hot, humid, long, and powerful ceremony. In it, the students are the only people seated on stage. They conduct the visitors in, welcome to the speakers to the podium, take their diplomas, and then leave on their own. Neither the superintendent, nor the faculty, nor the school board present them to the public wrapped in black and gold. Instead, they present themselves. "Here we are," they say, "for better or for worse, we are the best this community could do. You have committed the future to us."

The seniors may think, in their adolescent rhapsody of self, that the graduation is all about them. Later, they will learn that it is all about us out in the audience. We come to bear witness to the passing of time.

Only the bored and the morose measure time in weeks, days, hours, and months. Those who have hearts measure it in children. We mark it on the door jam, we put it on the refrigerator, we fill our photo albums, and we load our hard disks with time passing.

On island, those graduates are our best work. Eighteen years of hard work brought them to the door they stand before. We who live in the September and October of our lives, transferred the best of us to those who are in the April and May of theirs.

In the twenty-first century, we have so little to give them for their time. We don't give our children farms or businesses. We don't live in a hive of grandparents, uncles and aunts. We don't live in our father's towns and, in many cases, our children don't even live near their fathers. We teach them a little bit of wisdom, we make them listen to the Red Sox, and pat them on the back.

On stage, we see them as others will see them. They can see now, too. Those children who screamed, pouted, and broke curfew now see the door in front of them. The door may open to college, it may open to work, it may open to the French Foreign Legion, but it opens. For our part, the time to teach is over; they will be good fathers, they will be good mothers, they will be stewards of the island and voters and selectmen and yacht club commodores, if we have done our job well. The graduates on the stage have slipped from our grasp now and the moment on the stage is the last moment we have before they are gone from our hands.

Thankfully, June is not only the month of graduation, but also of reunion. Yesterday's graduates return to the island and their childhood bedrooms. They sleep late, they have bad haircuts, and they stay out deep into the night. But they are back with us. Later in life, they will come back with husbands, children, dirty dishes and attitude, but they come back. Safe in their rooms, or squabbling with their spouses, the floors sound with their voices and their feet and time stops.

Nantucket can seize time. Our clock seems glacial, certainly compared to mainland America's. Time hasn't changed the beach, the Juice Bar, Henry's Jr., the cobblestones, or the moors. Those new changes that appear in June seem only to be rearranging the deck chairs on a stationary ocean liner.

Had I a summer house, like many of those on Baxter Road, I would like to throttle time. I would like my parents, cousins, brother, sister, and children, to return to the house every year. They can track sand in, leave empty beer bottles on the porch, switch the radio station to Rush Limbaugh, and sleep in the mildewy sheets. We can leave the march and creep of time to the mainland, and we can hold the calendar, and our children, still.

It's a steep bill to stop time. They still don't give away the tomatoes at Bartlett's or the linen at Marine Home Center. When they come, child or father, aunt or cousin, they bring all of the annoyances and noise of their lives. Their cell phones chatter, their husbands annoy, and their advice, wrong headed. The floors may sound with their feet again, but it doesn't need to be at two in the morning.

Still, those who have graduated have come back now. They rest lightly in our hands, for as long as they are here. We cook the long, slow meal through the heat and humidity of the afternoon. In the glow of the evening, we eat the soup, the swordfish, and the apple cobbler as the sun closes in on the horizon. We hold by releasing, and we give so that we may keep this one moment.

10: The Well-Kept Hedge

Close friends of mine are lucky enough to live in one of the right addresses. As a result, nine months out of the year they have no neighbors within a well-struck two iron. In the summer, however, their street is a hive of activity. They tell a funny story of the new Nantucket. As the story goes, a new owner was visiting the house next to them and stopped by for a conversation. It was very brief; "We are going to grow the hedge two more feet. Your swing-set is too loud."

My friends related this story to me with a smile and I returned the favor. I have gotten used to this sort of behavior in May and June. The visitors come to look at their million-dollar sand castle and immediately establish a fortress of rights and privileges. They will park here, they will keep the music up loud, and they will mark off where they want the hedge to go.

The well-kept hedge symbolizes all that these people see. It marks their property line with a thorny wall. It hides the house, people, and view behind a natural barrier. The height of the wall indicates the depth of the checkbook. A neat, thick, healthy, and impenetrable hedge requires a lot of care and care is measured in dollars. Inside these green walls, the visitors can now watch television in peace, read e-mail from financial advisors, and pee on the rhododendrons. The final step in building a house on the new Nantucket seems to be encircling it in a hedge.

Hedges are nothing new out here, but they are the opposite of what Nantucket was. Nantucket has never been a private place. All of those Quakers were forever checking on each other for "disorderly walking." Those in-town houses were built tight to the street so that they could see everyone on the street and, conversely, everyone could see them. Good fences did not make good neighbors out here. Walking up Fair Street on a warm summer night was to tour through the families who live there.

The new visitors would call us "Nosy Parkers" and worse, but they aren't giving us credit. Nantucketers care about their neighbors. Visitors don't. The visitors come to the island with the belief that they have paid for the Gold Deck and should get all the privileges due them including the drink cart and the Captain's table dinner. Their neighbors on the Silver Deck or in steerage just don't matter. Cutting in line at Stop and Shop has no consequences to a visitor. They just get back inside the hedges sooner.

The beauty of the island has always been that visitors never last too long out here. You will need the good humor of the folks in steerage sooner than you think you will. It's an island; the people you snub will serve you soup or will come out to unclog a toilet. The visitors quickly learn that the way to get the plumber to come to your house quickly is not to cut him off in the check-out line. The visitors either learn this or they leave and go to the Vineyard. They love hedges over there.

Another friend has a neighbor who loves his lawyer. The neighbor sent over a legal cease and desist order to prevent blueberry picking. My friend laughed and sent over a pie. That winter, one of the visitor's skylights collapsed under the ice. Instead of laughing at the misfortune, my friend called the owner in New York, recommended a contractor, and plywooded the hole himself. During the next summer, they were barbecuing together. The Nantucketer's best quality is a concern for others. He teaches it as best he can.

I am afraid we have too few Nantucketers, too many visitors and we are putting up too, too many hedges. Many islanders have sold their lottery tickets and have moved to the woods of western Massachusetts and Vermont. Dozens of others look around, listen to the realtors and sell while they can. If history is any judge, many of them will regret giving up their place on our sandbar.

However, the island that they lived on has drifted into the past. The island of the future could be an island of more and more exclusive clubs where the richest of the plutocrats whittle down the membership lists into a platinum razor's edge of greed and jealousy. Each club will be its own green fortress, walled by hedges, and serviced by an off-island staff kept in employee housing. Edouard

Stackpole saw it in 1961. It will be an island of "caretakers, contractors, gift shops and lodging houses."

If Nantucket is to remain distinct from the Hobe Sound-Aspen axis, we need to fight those hedges. The wheeling flock of seagulls will always circle for the next best thing. When the island is appropriately parceled off into hedged-in squares, they will move onto the next open space and parcel that off in thorns. Our fortune doesn't come so much from the beach as from each other. As long as we keep looking out for each other, we will be Nantucketers no matter how high the shrubbery gets.

11: Independence Day

I spent Independence Day hiding. I wasn't in some top-secret bunker in West Virginia or hunkered down in the Naval Observatory, instead I clung to the beach at Sesachacha Pond with two little boys and several other families. A high haze faded out the sun, and a strong southwest breeze kicked up two-foot waves in the warm lake. The wind knocked over our beach chairs, tossed our towels into the dingys and sprayed sand in our faces.

Still, we enjoyed ourselves. My boys have invented dozens of water games to play with Poppa, including "motor boat," "rocky boat ride," and "Ferry ride." On the Fourth of July, "Ferry Ride" was our most popular game, as it involved thrusting each boy up and down each oncoming wave. Two hours of vigorous splashing, tossing, and bouncing left them punchy, exhausted, and ready to return home. That night, we avoided the fireworks crowd and went to spend fifty bucks at the carnival. On the way home, my youngest fell asleep in the back seat with sand in his toes and fried dough on his lips.

Most of my friends and acquaintances also declare their independence by either hiding or working. We avoid the Gordian Knot of downtown traffic by zipping off to the more remote corners and edges of beach and dune. In the past, the boys and I enjoyed the pleasures of the dunk tank, the pie eating, the bicycle parade, and the water fight. This year, the traffic was too daunting to attempt to engage. Ignoring it and hiding were the best options.

In the last ten years or so, Nantucket has been dogged by summer traffic problems. The cars pile up at the stop signs, be they at Five Corners, the high school, or, inexplicably, in the middle of Old South Road. The wise old salts deride the signs, as if the familiar red octagons somehow cause the problems. If we only removed the signs and the summer specials, they say, traffic would somehow flow naturally and holistically.

More likely, our growing traffic jams come from our growing construction. For thirty years, we have been biggering, and biggering, and biggering. We cannot put one hand out, saying "Business is business and business must grow" and then, with the other hand, complain about all of the cars piled up on Old South Road. If you don't build housing developments, you don't have car traffic.

For nine months of the year, traffic on island is not a problem, so most of us prefer to blame the tourists. The myth is that "Summer tenants bring five cars on island, including one for the nanny." If we blame the visitors, we can remain innocent and WE don't have to solve the problem. THEY do. Unfortunately, reality presents an inconvenient truth. The ferries have brought far fewer cars over to the island in the last seven years. In 1999, the big white boats carried 87,000 cars: in 2005, they carried 70,000. The cars that fill downtown in July don't spend the winter in Connecticut; they live in island garages.

Most of us see the problem of traffic as being as intractable as the weather. You can't change the fog on the Fourth and you can't change the traffic back-up to Henry's Jr. Like children, we are powerless to change something so big and vast. With a shrug and an "It is what it is," we duck out to Coatue. In the winter, when pressed, we will vote for well-meaning, but toothless, controls on other people's cars, write angry letters to the paper about our rights, and build more bikepaths and NRTA stops. Still, the water is getting noticeably warmer around our froggy feet. It may be that, as Churchill said, "the era of procrastination, of half measures…is coming to a close. In its place, we are entering a period of consequences."

This Independence Day brought other unwelcome traffic to the island. Portugese Men of War washed up in significant numbers on the southern shore. Normally, these nasty little beasts torment SpongeBob and Squidward in far warmer waters, but a long period of heavy wind from the south swept them up into our waters and closed the beaches for a day. Now, the old salts seem to remember a time when they swam side by side with these nasty little balls of stinging spaghetti. Perhaps this was when they went swimming after the whale that had Old Peleg's harpoon in it. I can't find too many mentions of Portugese Men of War in island history. Perhaps noone wrote about them because they were unremarkable.

Or perhaps the jellyfish, the southerly wind that brought them, and the warmer water that circles the island, are more signs of that natural inconvenient truth. The glaciers are melting all over the world, coral reefs are bleaching out, hurricanes are getting "power-ups", and the ocean currents are changing. The fishermen will tell you that the bass and bluefish arrive earlier and leave later, year by year. And the home insurance companies, when they send out the bill, will tell you that we are due for our own swirling gray lady.

In Churchill's words, we remain "resolved to be irresolute, adamant for drift, and solid for fluidity." We ignore the problem by hiding out at the beach, ignore it by pretending it has always been this way, or acknowledge it, and then blame others. Our traffic problems are caused by New Yorkers and global warming is caused by the Chinese. Throughout, we remain as innocent and as blameless as children.

Childhood ends. In the blueblack morning at the kitchen table, when sleep has fled and the bills are coming due, we list our options, sigh, and then pick up the tools. When I became a man, I put away childish things and picked up the tools of the world. A child is called to play in a world where there is no consequence: a man is called to the world of consequence to mend it. We don't mend the world by telling other people what to do or in pretending that there is no problem; we mend the world by fixing what we can fix in our own lives. You don't fix traffic jams by attending committee meetings, you fix them by leaving your car at home. You don't fix global warming by writing letters, you fix it by using less energy.

When Thomas Jefferson wrote the Declaration of Independence, he listed the grievances against the crown and then he declared the childhood of the colonies over. From that point on, we wouldn't shrug and say "it is what it is" or blame the crown for our own troubles. We wouldn't look to England to bail us out of trouble either. Washington, Boston, and Wall Street are not going to come down with a solution for our problems. We can't beg Daddy for the right answer. Jefferson, Hancock, and others swore their lives, their fortunes and their sacred honor in order to mend their world. So should we.

12: The Toypedo

The other morning I joined some friends in an early beach walk. We were on the south shore traipsing along in the fog. When you walk a beach, you absent yourself from the passage of time. Waves have always battered the shore of the land, whether humans, dinosaurs, or cockroaches walked the strand. Sand has always accepted the beating of the waves, morning, noon, or night. The Visa card payment schedule pales next a rolling set of combers.

I learned the trick of beach walking years ago. Don't walk near the water where the sand is soft, instead walk on the seaweed. I am sure that the elfin youth of little regard can dance like sandpipers along the edge of the sea, but once you become a man of substance, you tend to trudge like a moose. A firm pavement of kelp springs up under you like fresh sneakers.

In the past, when Nantucket was a truckstop between New York and Boston, such a walk would have afforded you a view of some of the finest ocean-going 18-wheelers of the age. Schooners and clippers would cross the horizon several times a day. And, several times a year, one of those trucks would jackknife in the sea and wash up in bales and beams onto the shore. Many of the island homes of that age featured beach treasures either in the roof, attic or front rooms. Today, you could probably find a few pressure-treated 4 x 4's and some coconut coir rope in the same place.

I have left far more beach treasures than I have found. Shoes, books, clothes, and sandwiches have all been left to the sea or the gulls. By myself, I am absent-minded. Add two boys and a supply train of juice boxes, toys, and clothes, and the possibilities of loss grow exponentially. Once, I lost my car keys in the sand. While my consort fumed beside me, I walked back to the beach, found where we had been sitting, and, to her amazement, fished the keys out. It would have been more amazing had I not been so practiced at it.

The boys have come of an age where they can do many of the things their father can do; they can swim, they can body surf, and they are very good at losing important things in the sand. At the dawn of summer, they went to

Sesachacha Pond with the wagon train of supplies. In a spasm of childish delight, they launched a tie-dyed toypedo into the murky water and gave it to time and the turtles.

So, our project for the summer has been a search for the toypedo. We grease the kids up, leave the house in the early afternoon, arrive in Quaise, strap our goggles on and hit the water. Within a minute, the usual water games commence and the search continues only with our feet. I doubt that our feet will find much; Davy Jones probably has a new pool toy. Still, stranger things have been spit back up from the sea and left on the beach.

A friend and colleague of mine, from long ago, recently popped up on Jetties Beach with her two boys pulling her along like kites. We let the children chase each other in the wind around the plover enclosure while we had coffee. Her life was pleasant, her children fun, and her tragedies mundane and human. She lived on St. Thomas, her husband designed wonderful houses for folks with wonderful bank accounts, and she had switched from teaching adolescents to dribble with the their left hand to teaching kindergartners not to dribble. I listened to what she said, but I kept hearing how she spoke and how she laughed.

Our memories do wonderful things, but they can't keep the whole of experience at our fingertips. We shorten things into brief little tabs and titles, then file it away. When I remembered her, I remembered in shorthand how she looked and what she had done. In the flesh, the short hand became music and the music swelled in her voice. Neither of us wished to travel back into that country of the past (unless it was to buy real estate), but we had both forgotten the treasures we had left there until the sea tossed it back to us.

In July, the island gives many treasures. The strawberries come in the early days of the month, as do the blackberries and bluefish. The fireworks flash several times over the sound, the wind turns to the southwest, the waves build, and the oldest continually running windmill occasionally grinds corn.

But I have come to appreciate finding old friends on vacation and walking the streets for a day or a week. I have come to an age when I can find former students, colleagues, and blood enemies walking pleasantly with an ice cream in hand and a smile on their faces. As long as they aren't living in my house for the week, it's great to meet them. While the times come back, the friendships do as well. The occasional dinner out is a small price to pay to find these folks again and to hear their voices.

However, now that I spend more time off-island, I have learned who the real beachwalkers are. When I come back to the island, I look for the old faces and voices of my past. I walk along the empty beach, next to the same waves that have rolled in, and will roll in, for millions of years. I look for the beach treasures I lost over the decades and wait to see what the sea will return to me, if anything. Home is the place where you wait for your toypedo to come back to you. And sometimes it does.

13: I Love to Beat You

On Wednesday, I stood amidst a thicket of blueberry and scrub oak, holding a silver horseshoe in one hand and a bourbon in the other. I set my hopes not to embarrass myself on the ground next to me.

Horseshoes has never been a game for me. Nor has bocce, volleyball, croquet, or softball. Unlike my host, I would never carve fifty feet of brush for a regulation horseshoe court, borrow the clay from a local tennis club, or light the whole thing for night-time play. But that didn't stop me from standing in the square and aiming the shoe at the 14-inch spike.

At that time, I was playing alongside a Canadian. Unlike those of us from the lower 48, this Canadian hadn't had a sense of shame or fear imprinted on him at an early age. Instead, he flung the horseshoes in roughly the right direction in between swills of beer. To our American chagrin, he managed several game-ending ringers. Luckily, also being Canadian, he had no idea he had won.

All our silly sports come out in the summer. The light lasts into prime time, the fog rolls in during the evening, and we find ourselves in the company of friends. When I was a kid, playing on Plymouth Road, we had to come in when the streetlights came on. Up until then, we ran through the yards of the neighbors fueled by Kool-Aid and Space Bars. Now, as an adult, we can stay out after the lights come on, but we no longer have the energy to run through the yards. Instead of tag, we play games that won't spill our drinks.

Four of us played spill-proof golf on Friday. Golf is much more to my taste, yet I have more affection for the sport than it has for me. We have advanced to a level where we don't embarrass ourselves on every hole and where, if we played and practiced a little bit more, we could really waste a lot of time away from those that need us. So much of our summer games seem to be such wastes of space, time, and money. George Carlin has a good idea; all of the golf courses should become house lots for the homeless. Yet, my Friday afternoons would be so much poorer for the new house lots. I spend much of the week looking forward to losing on the golf course.

Mark Twain was right; golf is a good walk spoiled. But, it is hard to find a better reason for that walk. My constitutionals around Miacomet give me the opportunity to send valuable golf balls into environmentally sensitive areas. Red Tail Hawks circle my errant drives. The sun sets on my grandmotherly putts. The ocean roars to my greenside shanks. Without golf, I could be of use; I could be cooking for my children, folding the laundry, or painting the fence. Instead, I am walking in the moors and wasting time and money.

Even that is too simple. Golf, horseshoes, and the rest of the silly summer sports have an intricate Virginia Reel of customs and rules. Most of those rules involve bragging rights. Losers walk off the court. You have to let the winner tee off first. You have to pay your debts right there on the golf course and you have to buy drinks afterwards . The winner can preen and look smug: the loser can taunt and mock. In my most recent match, the loser stuffed empty beer cans into the winner's golf bag. The winner, on the final tee, repaid the favor with poison ivy. On another round, we spent much of the round loosening each other's golf bags from the golf carts and laughing ourselves hoarse when the bag fell to earth. Even the Canadian enjoyed that.

It's just another outdoor game, it comes to little more. Every game of horseshoes, bocce, or golf is forgotten six hours after it was played. Very few men go to the nursing home with their Challenge Cups and Member-Guest trophies up over the TV. The dance of golf balls and horseshoes lasts about as long as every other dance does. Yet, noone dances for the sake of dancing. When we dance with our wives and our loved ones, we dance with them and for them. We don't dance in order to win or feed the kids or paint the fence. We dance because we love.

So it is with men and golf. In the words of Robert Frost, "by indirection, we find direction out." In our world, men can't look at each other and proclaim their love for each other. Instead of saying "I love you," we say "I love to beat you." It's far easier to sight a bocce ball, a thirty-foot putt, or a horseshoe than it is to proclaim affection. We parcel out our love in gimmes and two dollar Nassaus; we write valentines in score cards; we make presents out of poison ivy and crushed beer cans. The dance is the same at Sankaty as at Miacomet. Only the money and the drinks are different.

On Wednesday, I did embarrass myself. Slightly more than half of my tosses landed on the clay, never mind near the spike. I may have scored two or three points. Time will happily wipe that particular score card clean, as it has my golf, bocce, and croquet scores. Like the ice cubes in my tumbler, all of it will melt away in the heat of a July evening. As the darkness settles in around us, what remains are the voices of friends spun and woven into a rope that binds us together, even if it says "I look forward to crushing you again."

14: Drinking Champagne Every Day

I visited Nantucket thirty years ago. We normally vacationed on the Vineyard. After a few years of renting a house for a week, we began camping at the Martha's Vineyard Family Campground. Our summer vacations included long bike rides to the beach, sunsets in Menemsha, and wandering around Edgartown. On one of these trips, we got up early, drove to Oak Bluffs, got on the Naushon out of Wood's Hole, and sailed over to Nantucket.

It was a slow ride, which was perfect for us. We spread out our windbreakers and "sailed" over the deck. Later, we got the deck chairs going and sailed with them. As for my first visit, I am afraid to say that my memory fails me. I remember locking my brother in stocks at the old Gaol, but I am told that there never were stocks there. I remember the open moors, and the windmill, and the heat. There was a tour bus, of course, but it all blended together. In the end, we got back on the boat and sailed back for Oak Bluffs. Once there, my brother decided that he never wanted to leave and hid on the ferry. They held the Naushon at the dock for ten minutes while the crew went on a floor by floor sweep. He was found in the bathroom.

I sympathized with him then and I sympathize with him now. Leaving Nantucket is seldom pleasant or enjoyable. Deep inside, I have a secret smile during these last few weeks of August. The heat, the traffic, the crowds, and the various corporate pleasures await our visitors back on the mainland. They have to go, and I don't.

For the visitors, the last week is all about storage. Like squirrels, the visitors have to store their acorns for the winter. So, the sensitive figure out a last checklist of items: sunset, beach, swim in the surf, ice cream, donut, and pick up the paper. Then, with their bags filled with souvenirs and memories, they trudge back onto the boat and sail back to six lane highways and Happy Meals. My mother taught me about storing and hoarding. She came to the island for a week and brought home t-shirts and Glad bags filled with beach sand.

During the summer, the loud bray about congestion, lines, and prices. I suspect that, deep in their hearts, they would rather rake their own cherrystones than order them, watch the sunset of Madaket than over the 404, and watch the fog roll in during the peak of the heat. I know it in my heart; the prices of Target and Wal-Mart are nothing next to a good wave off of Madaquecham.

Sometime during that brief summer visit thirty years ago, I got sand in my shoes and kept finding myself back out here until I finally gave in and made it my home. Because of graduate school and a teaching schedule, I was moved back onto the island as boatloads of visitors were moving off. I arrived just in time. The corn was fresh, the tomatoes full, and the beaches were silent. The streets still held folks down for the weekend, or stretching themselves out into October, but the feeling and the conversation was decidedly past peak.

I know I am lucky. Living on Nantucket is like walking a golf course and finding ball after ball hidden the rough. You have only to look about you and find the treasures. In the morning, as we get the boys ready for school and usher them out the door, I can hear the far-off roar of the surf. At night, coming back from one tiresome meeting or another, my wife and I leave the car, look up, and see thousands of stars in clear Canadian air. Friendly faces knit themselves into the fabric of the day. Living on Nantucket is like drinking champagne every day. After a while, you forget how lucky you are to spend your life holding a wine glass. Our visitors know. They come, they drink the wine, and then they have to go.

Even if you are drinking champagne, you still know how fragile all of this is. Living on an island is living at the far end of civilization; we are an outpost in the Atlantic. On one hand, that means that everything we expect from civilization, from electricity to gasoline comes further and at greater peril and expense. On the other hand, we are that much closer to the elements. A roaring winter storm means more than a calendar page and a cocktail story when it surrounds you in February. We are at the mercy of the greedy, the stupid, and the arrogant both on island and off.

For the rest of America, the world breaks down into neat little walls and boundaries, either made by buildings, trees, or cubicles. Our visitors come here after having seen the world about them bordered in a frame. The frame could be a picture window, a windshield, or the yellow lines of the highway. Out here, Nantucket is surrounded only by the infinite. In every direction, there is only the straight line of the horizon. To go to Surfside and sit on the beach, even with one thousand others, is to put yourself before the infinite. No cathedral can shows man's relationship to God any clearer than that vast rolling shroud that washes up on Nobadeer.

Now that I am older, I understand my brother's need to hide in the Naushon's bathroom. Many things happen over the course of the year and there is no guarantee that you can ever return. The days spent on Nantucket are already gone as is the wind that cooled us and the waves we rode. Returning to the mainland is returning to voice mail, e-mail, memos, Wal-Mart, and the ten thousand things that clutter up the margins of our lives and put us back into the narrow frames of windshields and computer terminals. The visitors trade the infinite for the mundane. As I wave at the boat as it rounds Brant Point, I know that most of those inside are thinking the same thought; when can I get back?

15: A Cocoon of Fog

This evening the fog crept in on its little fog feet. From my back yard, the fog starts off as a dark blotch against the horizon, then the wisps blot out the houses in the distance, then it obscures the high brush until finally I can only make out the stone wall in the backyard and the blackberry bushes. The house cuddles into its cocoon of fog.

The fogs of July bring splendid isolation. The papers can't arrive, the phone service gets spotty, the air goes silent and, if you get lucky, the transformers short out. The electronic grid that supports modern society gets a little wobbly; Thomas Mayhew and his Madaket dugout isn't as far away as we thought he was.

In a few hours, the splendid isolation lifts and the neighbors make their reappearance. The realities of the twenty-first century return with the buzzing of the Cessnas and delivery of the Times. The cocoon dries up, cuddling time is over, and we get back to the business of our lives.

Nantucketers love their fog. Throughout our history, we have embraced the idea that we can put the problems of the present out there in the field and hide inside the warm, wet foggy confines of our houses. Perhaps those troubles will hop away like rabbits.

The list of modern ideas Nantucket tried to avoid is daunting. In 1878, we decided against town water. In 1884, we opposed a town sewer system. We opposed telephone wires and electric wires. We didn't want public schools and, later, we didn't want to build Academy Hill or the current high school. We only accepted automobiles in 1920 when the state forced us to. It took almost 25 years for the town to adopt basic zoning ideas to control growth. We thought Walter Beinecke was a dangerous loon. We voted against being represented in the Mass. Legislature. In the seventies, Senator Kennedy tried to make the island the equivalent of a National Park. We rejected that and chose to donate hundred of millions of dollars to conservation programs instead.

We love the past much more than the future. Scratch a Nantucket voter and he will tell you that things were better back then. In the present, we sail our way to hell in a lightship basket, but in the glorious past, hearts were truer, beer was colder, and the wind blew a gentle south westerly all year long.

Out here, this yearning for the past makes for entertaining cocktail chatter and long obituaries. It only comes to harm when it starts to affect our voting and our town leaders. Currently, it appears that we yearn for the halcyon days of the mid-eighties and nineties when wages were high, work was plentiful, and the overrides promising. If the fog rolls in nice and thick, we can drive on all of the beaches, get pay raises and no-show municipal jobs, find $50 an hour landscaping jobs for Junior and then sell grandma's house for 1.4 million.

If the fog burns off, we would notice that the island has reached a crossroads more perilous than any it has met since Maria Mitchell sat at her Dad's table in the Pacific National. Car traffic is choking both the streets and many of the beaches. The state is about to put the words "sewer moratorium" on our town seal. The island has grown so expensive that our children cannot reasonably expect to live here unless they become plumbers and like to live in our basements. Our older summer residents, who have bought subs and ice creams for children and grand children, are selling out for millions and moving to North Carolina.

The island has faced these problems before. Economic upturns (or downturns) have addressed them smartly. However, in the new millennium, it is no longer our island. Selectmen and the old families no longer hold the reins out here. Instead, Steve Karp, Bank of America, and Ralph Lauren are sitting in the front seat. We sold our birthright to these folks and now we are begging them to be nice to us. If you think Nantucketers still control much of island, I have a nice yacht club to show you.

The Plutocrats have a vision for the island. It's called Sconset. It will be a bucolic, timeless, beautiful community made up of billionaire golfers and their caddies. I know which end of the golf club I would be on.

If we want to continue to succeed out here and make a place for our kids, we are going to have to start looking more to the future than to the past. We were once a "barren sandbar fertilized only by whale-oil." We are still a barren sandbar, but tourists now do the office of the spermaceti. In order to keep the island vibrant, we need to keep the tourists happy. So, we may need to enact sensible limits on automobiles. We may need to regulate the beaches. We may need to manage the island's growth. But most of all, we need to look forward ten years or so and decide what we want the island to look like. Then we need to act.

But if we cuddle into the fog and forget what fertilizes the island, we will return to being a barren sandbar: someone else's barren sandbar.

15: Why Did We Ever Come Here?

The rain continues to fall.

Heavy rain does funny things to the island; there is no place for all of that fresh water to go, other than the ocean. But before it gets to the ocean, it puddles in the parking lots, cross streets and old pond beds.

Geologically, we are an odd place. Nantucket is one well-sculpted sand dune poking itself barely above the ocean water. Underneath the sand, however, is a tremendous bubble of ancient water, pushing itself up to the surface. Within yards of the briny deep, we have freshwater ponds. And, as the deluges of spring continue, those ponds overflow their calendar perfect banks and slip into basements, crawl spaces, and wine cellars. Last year, Miacomet pond finally overtopped the barrier beach and drained into the Atlantic, leaving a few inches of water, dead perch, three feet of muck, and two gigantic Koi flapping about. Two quick rainstorms and a good southwest wind refilled the pond so that the Koi, like developers, could continue to devour their home.

To me, and most of the year-round contingent, rain is merely another annoyance. It keeps the kids inside, closes up the job sites, fills the bars downtown, and leaks in the west-facing windows. But for the visitors who count each day as if it was a rosary bead, the rain steals money and time. The family stands downtown in raincoats and shorts, dodging from toy store to ice cream to museum to video store with one furtive eye on the sky.

I remember those days well. When I was green and wild in my youth, the parents brought us on vacation to the Vineyard. In order to prolong our stay and save money, we stayed in a gigantic tent. Bedouin living was fine in good weather. We bopped to the beach in the morning, showered and played softball in the late afternoon, grilled in the evening and fell into a salty, sandy sleep on an air mattress.

But when the rains came, tent living became a precarious, soggy nightmare. You couldn't touch the sides of the canvas tent for fear of causing leaks. Trenches, dug with admirably energy by my younger brother had to be redug and fortified, otherwise the water would pool up under the groundsheet. Everything inside the car stayed dry, everything inside the big tent got damp, Everything under the flap filled and flopped with standing water. You haven't lived until you have eaten soggy cereal in a limp paper bowl on a wet picnic table for dinner.

We spent the rainy days sitting in the main building shooting bumper pool, reading, playing interminable board games inside the damp tent, or driving from one town to the next in search of a cheap indoor amusement. Well within our earshot, my mother often wondered why we ever came.

Like most of my mother's questions, I only started thinking about it seriously once my hair turned steely. The older I get, the wiser my mother gets. My memory is only now letting go of her experiments in yogurt making, Transactional Analysis, and garbardine vests. With her dumb ideas getting boiled away in the try-works of time, her wise oil will remain.

Thirty years later and twenty miles to the south-east, other parents must ask the same questions. The intervening thirty years has given us great wonders. Now, instead of bumper pool and cribbage, the kids can watch "Dumb and Dumber" on DVD, listen to their iPods, text message their friends, and play Halo 2 marathons on the X-Box. It never rains on Super Mario Sunshine. Children are now household appliances. Plug them in, keep them fed, and show them off to the neighbors. My mother's questions echo and reverberate in the new millennium of personal electronic amusement parks; "Why did we ever come here?" We could plug the kids in more cheaply at home.

We came here because of "here." Nantucket has held itself back from the ebb tide of consumers and corporations. As a result, the island remains different from America. Debit cards won't buy you lunch, someone just baked the rolls your sandwich is on, and the lobster salad wasn't designed in a test kitchen. Anonymous American life is stuck in Hyannis with the traffic lights. Even with a billion dollars in real estate sales and three cable channels, we remain the "little town that time forgot." Everyone who returns to Nantucket comes to find their own lighthouses and channel markers: Cisco Beach, Bartlett Farm, Altar Rock, Great Point, Striped Bass at sunset. Then, with the compass and chronometer reset, they can return to the world of touchscreens, PIN numbers, and Zip Code marketing.

We came here, then, because it wasn't home. Home has bills, soccer practice, and drive-time DJ's on the radio. Home comforts us in an endless box step: work, kids, store, bed, then slide back to first position. A vacation not only ends the music, it tosses you off the dance floor. For better or worse, there you are with the spouse and the kids looking out a rainy window. Whatever you are going to do, it is going to be different from what you did last week or last month.

Or it should be. The Personal Electronic Amusement Park has its attractions, particularly for the parents. But the kids can watch "Old School" at home while you do the box step. Vacation might be a good time to listen to what the kids are listening to (briefly), drag them to things they don't want to see, and walk places they don't want to go. Even in the rain. At the very least, it will give their thumbs something to write.

My mother's question answers itself. We came here so that my family could become a "we" again. An overweight, over-sugared, bored, and damp "we," mind you, but a unified group nonetheless. On island, the family goes skating together, goes to the Maria Mitchell Aquarium, visits the Lifesaving Museum and drives to Sconset for ice cream and a view of the waves breaking on the Rose and Crown shoal. Off island, the family spins about on a child's mobile, circling the circles. On island, and in the rain, the spinning stops and the strings break. We are left with the only things we really ever have; each other.

Soon enough, the rosary beads and credit line will run out and we will have to return home. As sure as death and taxes, the last day will be one of transcendent clarity and warmth. With the car packed and the kids belted into the back seat, we will drive to the boat and hear, in the far off distance, the breakers rolling into the beach, the golf balls flying off the tee, and the sails luffing in the southwest breeze. Next year, we can enjoy this. Again.

17: The Luxury of August

My father is in Italy this August. He is visiting his sister, touring Tuscany, having drinks on the Piazza San Marco in Venice, then cruising the Adriatic. He will eat the finest gnocchi, he will see *Aida* in a coliseum, he will drink wonderful local wines, he will spend the inheritance and he will enjoy every moment of it.

For him, this trip, and his other recent European trips, harken back to vacations his father had taken him on. They would load the Cadillac on a trans-Atlantic liner, sail to Genoa, and drive around Italy. Once he was married and with children, the Grand Tour got shelved for my mother and her ideas of a practical and cheap vacation camping on Martha's Vineyard.

My mother loved beaches, although she hated swimming. On the calmest beaches, on the most windless days, she could be encouraged to enter the water for a gentle float and paddle about. All the while, she wore goggles, bathing cap, ear plugs, and nose plugs. Otherwise, she sat in her beach chair with its green and yellow umbrella and read trashy novels. She hated Italy and the Sommelier Luxury that went with visiting there. She would rather drink 'Gansetts under her umbrella and watch her children fling crabs at each other.

One morning, my mother and I left our campsite and pedaled eight miles to Oak Bluffs and East Chop Light to watch the sun rise. Neither of us anticipated the distance and we missed the sunrise by a good half hour. But we enjoyed the view, enjoyed our accomplishment in spite of ourselves and our miserable bikes, and enjoyed each other. Before we left, she snapped several pictures of Queen Anne's Lace by the side of the road, then she took me to breakfast at the Black Dog.

My mother saw Queen Anne's Lace as a rare wildflower. On vacation, she would stick a few sprigs in water for the picnic table. Later, she would press them into her books. Those pictures she took that morning on East Chop were blown up into eight-by-tens, framed, and hung in the living room. After she died, the pictures were replaced. Now, after my father has sold the house, I suppose they only live in my memory.

Queen Anne's Lace also lines the path to Sesachacha beach. I thought of my mother as I trailed my two boys to the beach one Sunday morning in August. One boy ran trailing a boogie board behind him. The other followed and tried to jump on the board so that his brother would drag him. When he eventually succeeded, both boys fell into a giggling heap, only to be beset by an affectionate basset hound.

Eventually, we established a base camp and then ventured into the tepid, still bathwater of the pond. The boys splashed each other mercilessly, then dunked each other. They pressed their father to either carry each on his shoulders, or to lead them in a game of "motorboat" or "rocky boatride" and, finally, to heave them into the air for a wet landing.

After forty-five minutes of amusement, I returned to the sand and the relative peace of the beach chair. The boys joined other Lost Boys in building the perpetual sand castle on the banks of the pond. They put in a race track and a heliport.

We were deep in the luxury of August. A breeze blew off the Atlantic, ruffling the water and swaying the beach grass. Far to the south, a line of plum-colored smoke rose up in a distant fog bank. Over the mainland, big, puffy fair weather clouds blew out singly over the water. The dragonflies paused in the beach grass. Constellations of terns swooped over the water. Others darted, then hovered, then dove after silvery fish.

Four swimmers had left the beach for the far shore and were now coming back at an easy, loping pace. Seven or eight families lined up their tents and towels over the sand. One enterprising group of young girls set up a table near the entrance for lemonade and chocolate chip cookies. The ladies with the big hats worked the blackberry bushes close to the road. I bought a cookie, opened my book, and watched the sand castle construction.

The island spends the month of August drunk on sunshine. It is a month without questions or diets or budgets. We read the newspaper or watch the news for heat waves, hurricanes, and horrors while we eat striper and shake the sand out of our flip-flops. The secret we smile at one another is that we are born lucky; lucky to be on this island, at this moment, and with these people.

Most of us realize that August ends. The wind comes down from the northwest, blowing Labor Day with it. Classrooms, offices, and snowstorms await. The run of good luck that has led us to this beach will fade into overtime, heartache, and boredom. Our day at the beach will disappear into the mush of yesterdays. Next year, the boys will want a surf beach. Next year, we may be working. Next year, all of us may not be back.

My mother and I didn't ride out to East Chop again. Time, tide, bills, and family conspired against us. We had other moments, of course, and other Augusts, but none of them were out at dawn with the Queen Anne's Lace. The Luxury of August cannot be stored or transferred or recreated or relived; it rushes by us in a torrent. It only remains in photographs, waistlines, and the half-remembered echoes we leave our kids after we have crossed over the bar.

My father may hear his father in Italy, somewhere. He may hear him in the roll of the ocean liner, in the roar of the car, or in the clink of the wine glasses in a roadside trattoria. I hear my mother in the breeze over Sesachacha. She brings the puffy clouds, ruffles the water, and tells me to have another cookie. It's August.

18: Enduring

August drifted onto the island in a fog bank. The water beaded up on the screens, wet the car seats, and mildewed the walls and ceilings, once again. All that summer promises comes due in August. Rain and polarfleece are banished; we finally receive beaches, blackberries, bluefish, and Bartlett's corn. For the visitors, the days are filled with sunscreen and sandwiches, the nights with cicadas and katydids.

Among the banks, realtors, and shops, the catechism reads "Let August be August." The sins of a slow spring and a slothful July are forgiven in the virtues of an industrious August. This August has begun piously enough. The restaurants are filled, the beaches are busy, and the water is in high demand. The waves roll in, the golf balls fly off, the ice cream is scooped out, and the cash drawer fills.

For year-round residents like myself, August brings traffic and trouble. The side streets fill with other cars and the main streets fill with bicycles that won't get out of our way. The lazy college kids quit their jobs and have beach parties with roaring fires while our kids stay home tying flies or go out star-gazing with their friends. The restaurants have raised the price of burgers and beer, forcing us to raise our own prices to match it. And those summer people set their sprinklers to water their yards in August, crashing our fragile water company and frying the pumps.

"Enduring August" has become the locker room chatter of the island, as if the locusts descend for the entire month and savage the place. Whenever we talk of traffic controls, we put it off saying, "it only affects us two months of the year." The same choir sings the same song for building limits, sewer systems, phones, electricity, and water pumps. The locusts come, we survive the onslaught, and the island returns to normal.

Other islanders see August as the season of the big fish. When you can sell a bottle of Cristal for as much as four cases of Budweiser, why stock beer? If you can sell a filet for $50 or a burger for $10, you should sell the steak; one person in one seat for one-and-a-half-hours. The same goes for room rentals or house rentals; you charge what the market will bear. However, when you stop seeing customers as people with kids and friends and start seeing them as full beds and warm seats, Nantucket becomes just as nameless and faceless as anywhere else. And anywhere else is a lot cheaper.

I have been off-island twice so far during the month of August. Distance from the island allows a clearer perspective on our virtues and our vices. More to the point, I could see our golden sandbar as our visitors do.

The blessings of Nantucket never quite seem as rich as they do when you stuck in traffic on Route 84 in 90 degree heat. The promise of Cisco beach is a lot richer than the promise of the pool at the Day's Inn. Applebee's, Macaroni Grille, and TGIFriday's have the same bland, corporate food that looks great on presentation but hangs on the tastebuds like cheesy, salty dust: The Stepford community of the "Shoppes at Farmington Valley" has more in common with the mannequins than the people in them. I have never felt more like a representative of a zip code than I did at the

Barnes and Noble's Recommended Readings table. All of those people waiting in five miles of cars on the other side of the Bourne Bridge were there for a reason; they were fleeing marketers and humidity. They are willing to pay the price.

But what a price. Off-island, my wife and I got to see what Americans actually pay. We got the Wal-Mart experience. Wal-Mart may be the corporate sinners and health care raiders of the modern world, but they do sell cheap stuff. Our moment of cultural cognitive dissonance came in front of a display for ballpoint pens. They were selling 24 packs for a dollar. Like Yeltsin in the Houston supermarket, we couldn't accept the reality. Ma and Pa Kettle came to the big city and got dazzled. Four mixed drinks on Nantucket bought a full dinner at Bertucci's, a nice room at a bed and breakfast cost less than a round of golf at Miacomet, and an entire bedroom set at Ikea cost less than a dinner for four at one of our high end restaurants. If I got sticker shock in America, what must all of those Americans think when they come here?

Nantucket is busy outpricing itself. All of those middle class families that came here for a week or a month have got to be looking anywhere else. Four hundred bucks for the car to come over, three thousand to rent the house, five bucks for an ice cream and six bucks for a draft. Splurging is one thing; hemorrhaging money is quite another. Out here, we shouldn't need a historian to realize that summer is no longer summer, July is no longer July, and August has shrunk down to two busy weeks. The Jersey shore, the coast of Maine, and even the Canadian Maritimes look pretty appetizing and affordable.

And yet.

After I returned home, I went to Madaquecham for a few hours. At a brief and easy walk from the car, I set up the chair two hundred yards away from the nearest folk. Warm water rolled in, relatively cool air blew, and the only human sounds came from a pair of Kadima paddles somewhere down the beach. I-84 in Hartford was a bad dream.

Three couples and a brigade of kids encamped. The kids boogie-boarded and bounced in the waves, they threw Frisbees and built sand defenses and drink juice boxes. The adults sat in their chairs, eyed the kids, read their books, and soaked up the sun. It was as it had always been. They had come here, they had paid the price and August was August.

And they will keep coming back, and their kids will keep coming back as long as we know why they come and we respect it. The family that visits for a week is our family; the money that they spend could be our money. If we make decisions about Nantucket that look at what we would want as opposed to what the market will bear, we will continue to be successful. If Islanders see the visitors as big fish, full tables, or locusts, they will start looking for anyplace else. And anyplace else is a lot cheaper.

19: Let August Be August

"Let August be August," they asked.

The winter had overstayed its welcome and pushed spring into a long weekend. Boat reservations and gas prices and rents and yields and bonuses foretold an ominous time. They had spent the winter stuck in traffic at the mini-mall, dreaming of the island.

Time had moved the island. The old couple had sold their house next door for a mint. They wouldn't be dropping off tomatoes or watching the kids from the porch. The summer house needed paint. Some pipes had frozen upstairs. There was talk about selling the field behind the house. It was different. The cars and the prices and the lawyer-neighbors and the taxes....

But they filled the Escalade, bought a dozen donuts, and drove. They stopped at McDonald's one last time, for the kids, and then, up the ramp and onto the ferry. They left the backseat full of trash and they roamed the upper decks. They stood in the wind and surreptitiously searched for lighthouses and headlands.

When they arrive, it IS August. It is the season of ripeness; it hangs heavy from the branch. The slightest touch drops it into your hand. A bite brings the accustomed incomprehensible sweetness. It is as good as last year: corn, blackberries, lobster, tomatoes, steamers, zucchini, littlenecks, and ice cream. It is the best they ever had, again.

These are the days when Death is nowhere. "These are the days that go from joy to joy to joy, from blossom to blossom." The diet is unnecessary, the budget is forgotten, and the workout plan rationalized into walks on the beach and tennis with the nephew.

When they wake up, the silence unwraps them into a roll of surf and a whisper of breeze. Someone bikes off for donuts. The newspapers had yet to make it through the mist. Plans are made. The clutter is organized into piles.

Reservations are called into tennis courts, golf courses, and restaurants.

Then, to the beach. They wear their wet swimsuits and bring their towels from the clothesline. Perhaps they bring surfboards and fishing rods and swimsuits bought in the sleep of winter when August was a dream. They park up close and carry it down to the sand and sit with their eyes on the horizon. The beach fills their heads and lungs with sand, salt, and Bain de Soleil. They come with Cheese Specials and Kadima, with bestsellers and dump books then proceed to dust it all with sand.

It is the best beach. It has a sandbar twenty yards off shore, perfect for bodysurfing. The waves break in formation, all the way down to Nobadeer. The water has warmed into the seventies, which means a pleasant shock on the way in, and then a rolling, warm torpor. The terns dart amid the waves. The cumulus hikes through the noonday sky.

They build sand castles, with moats, towers, and defenses. They pick up shells. They join the kids on sandbar and let an ocean wave crest and carry a winter of indulgences and chocolate into the beach. They nap. They read. They drink Narragansetts and listen to the Sox game.

They have time. In the afternoon, there is time to find golf balls that didn't have smiles and play nine at Skinner's. There are tennis rackets still in presses and tennis balls that have a little life left in them. There is time to get the day-sailer ready and cruise over to Coatue. There are bikes that didn't need locks and there is a brief walk to town for soft-serve ice cream and pixy sticks; for atomic fireballs and bull's-eyes; for Grisham and Philbrick and *People*.

And they have time for the backyard. They have time for the hammock and the Adirondack chair. There are swifts, starlings, and swallows. The hawks patrol overhead and, far up in the blue of the sky, the gulls circle. The high grass and Queen Anne's Lace blow in waves over the field. The hydrangea buttresses the house with the Black Eyed Susans, the Morning Glories, and the Beach Roses. Croquet mallets and wiffleball bats stand sentry while escaped soccer balls and Frisbees hide in the bushes. They could garden. They could read. They could write letters. They could nap.

When dinner comes, it brings striped bass or swordfish on a bed of coals. Gin and tonics in plastic glasses join beer bottles and white wine on the counters, picnic tables, and stone walls. The evening is made for buckles, brambles, and cobbler, with a dollop of vanilla ice cream.

Perhaps they go to a movie. Perhaps to a concert. Perhaps to a lecture. Perhaps to a beach party. Perhaps they stay home on the sofa, with the TV or the radio and that same old book. The fog walks up the path and settles into another humid, sleepless night of sand in the sheets and salt on the skin.

And so it goes. They "hold infinity in the palm of their hands and eternity in an hour." Time lets them play and be golden. They measure their days in auctions and benefits, tee-times and regattas, house tours and benefit cocktail parties.

Sometime after the Pops concert, they start to hoard the memories. They buy a t-shirt and a calendar, collect some sand in a bag, develop the pictures, and store up those bits of flotsam that will need to last through another Connecticut winter. Soon, they are closing the shutters, emptying the refrigerator, draining the pipes, and packing the Escalade. The inexorable gravity of courtesy, contracts, and classrooms tugs them away. As they stand on the deck of the ferry, they toss the penny as they always do. Looking backwards, they sail into their future of highways, stoplights, and mini-malls.

"For another year, August was August," they sigh.

20: Cobbletones

A few days ago, I stood outside Zero Main and watched the final Cobbletones performance of the summer. Probably a hundred well-fed and wallet-lightened visitors mixed in with the parents and girlfriends to watch the eight sing for the last time. The air was warm, the moon was just coming out, and we all felt lucky to be there.

The calendar had caught up with the singers and painted them in sepia. It was one of those Last Times. The eight boys stood at the base of Main Street and worked their way through the glee club staples, a cappella. The performances were stuffed with more than the usual inside jokes. But it would be the last performance for at least one of the boys. Several cried on Caleb Wheldon's final version of "The Superman Song." Then they sang their last song and we all walked into the night.

One of the more unpleasant things I have learned as an adult is that you always go walking into the night. We leave golf partners, co-workers, and mortal enemies back in the darkness. We don't mean to. We collect addresses, sign yearbooks, and even keep the phone numbers, but time and tides split those best intentions away from Visa-paying, child-crying reality. Those names reproach us from the datebook and appear on the Christmas card list.

For the most part, that is a hard but necessary step. High school championships fade months after they are won. We want our kids to move on into the wide, wide world. We want them to be happy and fulfilled and successful. Singing on a street corner is a great lark when you are 22. By the time you turn 40, it has gotten a bit old.

That's what we knew when we watched the Cobbletones sing their last time. We knew that this would be it. There would soon be college degrees, rewarding careers and wives. In spite of promised reunions, this would be the end of that era. As way leads onto way, we doubted if we would ever come back.

But that is one of the things about Nantucket; it seems that we can always go back. If the God's punch-clock is going to stop anywhere, it will probably be here. The island goes out of its way to measure time geologically. The grass grows, the sand either wears away or builds up, the paint peels, and there are different flowers in the fountain on Main Street.

Nantucket has been very good about keeping the sign posts the same year to year. The great wealth that the island enjoys comes from the stools at the lunch counters and the chewy crust to the Portugese bread. Our visitors come off the boat and re-enter last year. All of those people who have drifted out of our lives, drift back in. Time stops.

As I lead walking tours around Main Street, I carry a bag full of N.H.A. photos from years gone by. I stop in three or four spots, hold the picture up and ask the visitors to compare. The photo and reality are so similar as to be cousins: perhaps there are wires, perhaps there are cars, or perhaps the road is now paved. But the scene is the same.

The tourists on the beach have descended deep into Brigadoon. The beach only knows the months, not the years.

Waves, horizon and clouds: The water warms slowly and the sandbars form. Perhaps there are more people now and they bring more toys and less fabric. If you replace the cell phones with transistor radios, you could hopscotch across the generations.

Of course it's not true. Of course it is an illusion. The real estate and the obituaries give the lie to that precious little dream. In spite of the washing of the waves and the spinning of the windmill, boys become fathers and fathers become grandfathers.

But those of us who live here have a relatively timeless existence. We haven't seen a subdivision grow in the middle of a field during six months nor have we witnessed the branch office go through three different signs in two weeks. In a world where buildings and towns rise and fall in months, an island where the donuts haven't changed in decades seems too good to be true.

That's why the visitors all come here. They all want to slip back into a timeless bubble. The Washington lawyers wish to sit on a Main Street bench and get ignored.   The workout millionaires want to go for jogs in the moors. The Wall Street thieves want to write checks for their dinners. They know that the earth, the clock and the calendar will keep spinning. For fifty weeks a year, time marches through their day in billable hours, appointments, and electronic reminder beeps. For two weeks, it can stand under the moonlight and listen on the street corner.

They want to believe that Nantucket is special and timeless, at least in August. So, they want to believe that sometime next July, eight boys will reappear on a street corner and start singing "It's Almost Like Being In Love."

I share their hope. I just hope it isn't the same eight boys.

21: Bricks for the Basement

The houseguests come in September and they blacken the walls like mildew. We invited them down in the months when the snow blew up against the glass and it seemed like a good idea to reconnect with Cousin Billy and his family. When the day and ferry finally arrive, we welcome them with clenched teeth and crossed fingers. A good houseguest arrives with a bottle of bourbon, a bag full of steaks, and an urge to wash dishes. And then stays as long as it takes a fish to go bad in the fridge.

Recently, we entertained a very old confirmed bachelor, my Uncle Oswald. He babysat the kids, played in the surf, and read them stories at night. Oswald gave them airplane rides in the backyard and shoulder rides in the waves. In short, he was a wonderful houseguest for two busy parents. But he had no desire for kids of his own. None. Now, he will have an obituary that many of us would envy. He has a law degree, a teaching degree, can order drinks in four languages, and has been on a ski patrol in Switzerland. Uncle Oswald performs in local theater, plays violin in an orchestra, and rides a horse for relaxation. He is comfortable enough in his own skin to laugh at his own eccentricities.

But he hates the ice cream truck. It drives through his neighborhood in New Jersey every afternoon and never at a regular time. The truck plays the familiar, loud, tune over loudspeakers that calls the kids to come running. He has had long, ranting tirades at the driver, he has complained to the police, he has written letters to the paper, and he has tried to get the neighborhood to sign a petition. Still, it comes.

As a parent, I laughed at his jokes, drank his bourbon, and knew that I spoke a language he couldn't understand. His kids wouldn't run out the front door for a Firecracker Popsicle, nor would they draw the ice cream truck on scrap paper, nor would they remember that annoying song fondly for decades. Nor would he ever walk out to the ice cream truck, hand over the exorbitant sum, and wish, somehow, that you could hold that moment, and that popsicle, frozen in time.

Having children is like drinking champagne every day. Sometime the champagne is tremendous, sometimes it is gutter swill, and it is there every day. You get used to it after a while and you don't really notice the taste, until you get an odd moment of clarity and you think 'My God, I am drinking champagne." Then, you also know that you will never drink from this glass again, and you may never remember this brief shining draught.

One day, recently, my two boys and I went to Children's Beach. As is true in July, the parking lot was full, the beach was crowded and the water still, tepid, and murky. Both boys ran to the water, jumped in, and proceeded to splash each other silly. Then, they joined up with another boy and gave each other rides on a boogie board. One would pull, one would ride, and one would try to trip them up. The boy with the boogie board went in for a snack and another boy, smaller and more reserved, joined up with my two ruffians for their "Rescue Swimmer and the Shark" game. I stood on shore and watched, hoping that everyone would keep their bones unbroken and their lungs free of seawater. I was joined on shore by the boy's mother, who wore a full, brown burka. The two of us shared very few cultural codes, but we did share a bond of parenthood. We both wanted to go in the water and calm them down, but we both knew that we shouldn't.

My children make me be a better person; it isn't something I would do naturally. They make me hold me tongue, wash my hands, sit up straighter, and wear a seatbelt. They pull me out of my comfortable, cynical shell and leave me singing and dancing around in a circle. With the same eyes that mooched free donuts, my youngest got me into the circle around Susan Salidor. We sang, we danced, we hopped up and down, and we clapped as the song called. My wife was in hysterics; yet the youngest wanted Daddy to sit with him. And so I did.

My children believe that miracles happen every day. It becomes my duty to insure that they occur on schedule. When we were at the beach at Quidnet, my oldest asked about the skate egg cases that were enmeshed in the seaweed. I told them that they were Mermaid's Purses. So, promptly, they started breaking them open to see what sort of money mermaids used. Later, as they were attempting to create a sand castle, they discovered sand fleas. They collected them in the moat of the castle, then bid them good sailing as they got swept out to sea on a vigorous wave. In the last dip of the day, my youngest lost a toy in the waves. Clearly lost forever to Davy Jones' Locker, we consoled him on his loss. As we left the beach, however, an older gentleman jogged up behind us and returned the toy. The wife and I were stunned, but the boy was not. He sees miracles every day.

To be a parent is to perform in front of an audience every moment. This audience has a phenomenal memory, yet may not remember anything from this moment twenty years from now. Every step and mis-step contributes to your child's character, but you have no idea what it will do. You just hope that it keeps his attention on you and not on Sponge-Bob. I give the hunt lecture at the Whaling Museum on many afternoons. A father and son came up to me after one of the talks when I didn't drop the harpoon or flub my lines; the father complimented the talk, saying that it kept his son's attention for the full forty-five minutes. I told him that I hoped his son would grow up to be a whaler.

When I think back on my life as a father, I think that so much of my time is designed to build the bricks of good memories. I know that they will never remember my dancing to "The Backwards Song" or the lost beach toy or even the primary diet of sperm whales. But I hope that each one of those memories becomes a brick in the foundation of their house. It will be up to him to build a good house, but if we can build a good basement, he will be well on his way.

Some of the most heartbreaking items in the whaling museum come from those whalers who spent years away from their children. Unlike my Uncle Oswald, they can speak the language, but they have no occasion to do it. A miniature ivory bed is in the scrimshaw room, complete with springs and an elaborately decorated headboard. Some whaler, in the middle of the Japan Grounds, sat on a deck reeking of dead whale and carved the ivory into a delicate doll's bed. He knew he couldn't give his gift for years, he knew he might die before he gave it, that she might die before she received it, or that she might break it or not be interested. His daughter may have been four when he left and may be eight or nine when he returned. Yet, he still carved a toy for her. He wanted this brick for her basement. Even though he wasn't at home, he wanted her to know that he loved her.

What that whaler knew, and what my Uncle Oswald doesn't, is that we measure our days in play. The only things that matter are the bricks that get built into a child's foundation. Whatever we value, whether it be Schubert or the Simpsons, will not last unless we somehow preserve it in the minds of our children. The bells of that truck will outlive the chimes of the Vatican.

22: The End of Something

Sometime last week, while I was busy throwing children at Jetties or losing golf balls at Skinners, the tide turned. Summer, which has been flooding the island for months, had come to slack water, and then, the boats swung on their moorings, and summer ebbed.

In the morning, the chill slipped in the screen doors and open windows and then slept on the sofa. The traffic on Crooked Lane has slowed, as have the terminal backups on Quaker Lane and Sparks Avenue. The bluefish and stripers are back and rising. The college kids have left suddenly and the owners are back behind the counter, throwing out jokes and shrugging at the line. The high school kids have discovered their summer reading and their Spark Notes as football and soccer double sessions loom just outside the harbor.

The final big events of the summer fall in these weeks. The Demo Derby reintroduces the islanders to each other, generally at high speed and in reverse. The Sand Castle contest fills the waterline at Jetties while Race Week glides over the sound. Then the boats and the sand architects take their place on the outgoing tide.

Summer does not end with a crash and a cocktail party. Rather, it slowly fades out until the parking spaces return to Main Street and the sidewalks and breakfast counters fill with familiar faces. The college kids leave their jobs with t-shirts and hangovers sometime in mid-August. Then, as Labor Day approaches, the families leave and go back to cubicles and classrooms. During late September, the Jupiter Island crowd tips the tennis pro, calls the caretaker, and drifts back down to Florida. The Weddings and Weekenders dribble out around Columbus Day and, by Halloween, the island is left to us. And we are worried.

All change is gradual, but the realization is sudden. The tide shifts sometime while we are busy with our cell phones and our sandwiches, and then, when we look up, the water and the hours are racing out of the harbor. Recently, the Taxi Driving Wise Men and the Barstool Prophets have noticed that the tide is running out on the tourism boom.

The real estate listings back up for months and the asking price slips downward. The boat carries fewer passengers and the restaurants seat fewer diners. Empty hotel rooms, empty rental houses, and empty stores dot the island like so many beached boats. The taxis and the barstools cluck and fret with worry.

They are right. The age of t-shirts, ice cream, and day-trippers has drawn to a close. In addition, the age of bringing the family for two weeks on the beach is also drawing to an end.

The bills have come due. The sewer bill stands in the doorway, followed by ones for trash, gas, electricity, health care, and food. Nevermind the spec house gambles, over-charged credit cards, and adjustable rate mortgages that brought Hummers and jet skis. Whoever is here in ten years will have to bring those expensive guests in and make them comfortable.

One constant in the history of the island is change. The beaches and the sands shift constantly; Sankaty wears away and becomes Tom Nevers. Cisco wears away and becomes Tuckernuck. Fortunes grow and melt, families come and go, and houses rise and fall. A rich man's house will be a barn in a hundred years and a barn will become a rich man's house.

I spent several days last week weighing down a bench at the Oldest House. The tour buses drove by, the visitors come up and get a tour through the building, but it is a quiet place by and large. The house was built by people who thought the wealth of the island would lie in wool, not oil. Those days, the island had more sheep than people and more people than trees; the world Jethro looked out on every morning was a bare Scottish golf course. Then, as whaling became profitable, the house was bought by the Paddocks. They built a secondary dwelling, rented a room to a whaling captain, and put 20 people up there. The men were out at the beach or away on boats, the hill was a commune for Amazonian Quakers. Then, as whaling faded and the Paddocks faded as well, the oldest house became a barn. Finally, in the late nineteenth century, the Coffins bought it, "restored" and retired it to spending its next century collecting tourist's footprints and photographs.

The house has seen sheds, barns, gables, and radical surgery at the back. The land around the house has seen roads, farms, gardens, and a Native American landfill. The trees have grown up around the house, including one of the last remnants of the island's silk industry, a large mulberry tree in the front yard.

The prophets and wise men stood in this yard and clucked many times. Jethro Coffin saw the wool trade failing and he moved his family off island. George Turner saw the demand for his barrels fall and switched over to farming. Now, we see fewer tourists walking through and driving past. What will become of us as the tide goes out?

The other great constant in the history of the island is community. No matter what has happened, from fire to drought to war to depression to boom, there has always been an "us." We have learned how to walk together, gone to school together, married each other, worked with each other, left and finally returned to the island. Rich or poor, young or old, we stop by for a visit, wave on the street, and connect.

Our new age features people who live on vast glaciers of wealth; they have names like Chappy, Biff, and Janette. They have wine cellars and air-conditioning. They bring chefs and have catered meals at their houses. They give each other monogrammed loot bags for housewarming presents after they fly in on a chartered plane from Amagansett. And still, they make a community. They visit the neighbors, stop in for a cup of coffee and for a gossip and philosophy omelet, then re-connect. Chappy and Melissa are not so different from Jethro and Mary. Or from you and me.

The Boom sets, the Boom also rises, but we endure forever. The community of Nantucket has remained throughout all those changes. Be it Native American, Quaker, or Capitalist, Nantucketers look to each other and their neighbors. The buildings don't make Nantucket a small town in the sea, the people do.

Were life to send me elsewhere for the rest of my life, I would not miss the Oldest House, the cobblestones, or the mansions on Baxter Road. Other places have oceans, moors, and cedar shingles. I would miss all of my neighbors and I would hold them in my heart, free from time and tide, and build my own Nantucket there.

23: Labor Day

Labor Day creeps towards us like a tardy schoolboy. The streets lose the human crush, the nights lose the mind-pressing humidity, and the shops lose their workers to pressing family emergencies. All across this great land, grandmothers choose this last week to succumb to illness, retreat to their beds, and call their children home from ice cream-scooping and bed-making to attend them in their hour of need. On Nantucket, the three most popular lies are "I'll be back right after lunch," "The striper was a keeper when I brought it in," and" I'll be here through Labor Day."

As a teacher, Labor Day had a far different connotation for me. Just as everyone else was gearing down into the shoulder season, I was gearing up for the school year. Labor Day came with pointless professional development and the low rumble of approaching buses. As the visitors left the Cape, I arrived.

September begins the push to June. Most of the teachers would come into school that Monday and set up their classrooms. We would bring out the textbooks, pilfer the supplies, steal the comfortable chairs from the Special Ed teachers, photocopy the class rules and brace ourselves for the rush. Soon our days would fill with students and our evenings with grading. Teaching has moments of transcendent grace and meaning but, for the most part, it is labor.

Just like any other job, of course. Sandwich-making is a dull, repetitive parade of cold cuts and mayonnaise. Carpenters spend a great deal of time sweeping and cleaning. Lifeguards get bored stupid staring at the waves. Robert Frost would have us believe that work should be "play, for mortal stakes." Perhaps he should pick up a broom and help us sweep up.

Labor Day isn't dedicated to sweeping and grading vocab quizzes; it is a day when we should put our vocations aside and reach for our avocations. Noone wants to be his job. We all wish to be a lot more interesting than a stack of grammar quizzes and ten dozen sandwich rolls. Our labor shouldn't be our lives. If you measure your days with a red pen, then you are neither serving yourself, your fellow man, nor God.

The Quakers, back during the heady glory days of Whaling, believed just that. Hard work and mindless toil did indeed serve God. In fact, the better you got paid, the better you served God. So, would be poets, like Peleg Folger, and painters and musicians were just out of luck. Drop the pen and pick up the whale line.

When we look back on the time of the Quakers, for the most part we are looking at shadows of a people, no more substantial than their silhouettes. Before the American Revolution, Nantucket was one of the economic dynamos of the country. A huge chunk of all of the money the British spent in the colonies got spent here. The Gardners, the Folgers, the Husseys, and the Rotchs became intensely rich. We have their checking account registers; we know.

We don't have any great murals, statues, fountains, buildings, or even poems from that time. The whole island followed the sinking star of Labor. Ten thousand people lived and worked here, but none of them left any trace of a hobby behind, not even a lost golf ball. Whatever they spent their money on, it wasn't fun.

They lived on the same island I live on. They stared at the great gray lid that came down in the winter. Without the temptations of cable, Playstation, and the internet, they must have had time on their hands. Even the boys out on the south shore who watch for whales must have had some way of spending their time, other than basking in the glow of their inner light.

Today, my happiest friends are the ones who don't let their labor get in the way of their passion. While they should reinvest the money they make in whaling ships, real estate, and tools, they instead buy mandolins and golf clubs. The shop teachers at the high school play bluegrass. The minister has a farm and a library in Old English. The carpenter is a fisherman and the plumber is a surfer. The peppergun guy is building his own plane. The surgeon is making arrowheads. The sailing instructor writes about Nantucket history. Two hundred years ago, the Quaker's passion was their labor. Today, it is hard to see the light of God in a stack of research papers or a clogged toilet, although it may be there. It may be a lot easier to find Him in an obsidian arrowhead or an ultralight plane.

Robert Frost wanted our passion and our labor to be "two eyes that make one in sight." Reality is a lot more cock-eyed. We labor in our day jobs. At night, or on the weekends, our hobbies and our passions lead us on. And, in the teeth of a foggy, wet, Nantucket winter, the heat of our passions keep us warm.

Hanna and Gertrude Monaghan had it right, I suppose. The two Quaker sisters came to Nantucket, bought an old pig barn, and converted it into a showplace for artistic passion. Their belief was that the light of God not only lit up the counting houses, candle factories, and whaling ships of the world, but also the studios, workshops, and gardens. God's Greater Light illuminated all honest labor, be it in candle-making or golfing. If you opened your heart and found God within, and he bade you speak truth, couldn't your truth be in the form of a painting as much as in a tract or in a barrel of winter press oil?

"Greater Light," on Howard Street, is closed these days due to a sagging roof. Inside, the house is a psalm of that God that we carry within us, whether as a carpenter or as a sculptor. The Monaghans brought in six gold-plated Italian pillars, a set of Venetian plaques, a harem curtain, and two huge wrought iron gates and saw the light of God made manifest in all of them.

Labor Day brings many things with it, not the least of which being the plague that affects grandmothers everywhere. Labor Day brings about the end of summer and the end to the eighteen-hour-a-day labor for the surgeon, sandwich maker, and sailing instructor. It also marks the beginning of passions, when we can finally pick up the mandolin and the golf club, and warm ourselves, this winter, in our Greater Light.

24: September Song

September is in the air.

Sometime at the end of August, a Canadian cold front slips over the Adirondacks and the Berkshires, fords the Connecticut River and then sweeps over the coast and the island. August's beer has become September's bourbon.

That cold air has swept the fog and the haze out to sea and brought back in cold nights and clear stars. The stripers are back, fat with pogies from Maine, and the tuna are chasing them. The corn is sweeter, the tomatoes still plump, and the apples redden on the branch. Fed by the swirling ladies of the Caribbean, the surf is up, cresting on an on-shore wind. Beach space becomes cheap again, as do parking lots, reservations, and court times. On a Wednesday morning, you can park next to the Bartlett's truck and spend a half hour on the bench talking baseball to Jack without smelling a cigar, hearing a cell-phone, or seeing any Lilly.

August has its charms. Business is great, the streets are filled, long lost friends come by, and everyone feels lucky. On Nantucket, August is one long beer blast. We are all here, jammed together with the rich and famous, dishing out the suds as fast as we can pump and cleaning it up in the morning. Even in the fog, the neighbors' houses are well lit, the cars are parked all over the yard, the towels hang sullenly off the lines, and the music goes into the wee hours. Like houseguests, August is welcomed for the excitement and the change, then it is gone. They pick up a calendar and some note cards on the way to the boat, leave a bottle of wine in the fridge, toss the penny overboard, and go back to Hartford.

On a beautiful Wednesday in September, they are thinking of us. They catch up on their voice mail and the stack of memos, but their mind is back on the beach and their eyes are on the photo in the calendar. They know that the golf course is nearly empty. They know that they can get into the Company of the Cauldron now. They know that Cisco has a six foot swell breaking on that long sandbar. They know that that little bit of irritation that the lines and the crowds caused is all gone. It would be perfect on Nantucket. And they are in Hartford.

Islanders have a hard time with perfection. We are always working. The families and houseguests aren't the only ones to leave at the end of August. So do the college kids and the high school students who pulled many shifts. Suddenly waitresses are working doubles without the benefit of the busboy. The ice cream store and t-shirt shop are still open late, but the islanders have come out from the office and put an apron on. School starts, tenants need to be found, fixes have to be made, on and on and on.

Work becomes its own excuse. Of course, we need to work. Someone needs to pay the bills and get the baby new shoes. But, the world is full of places where we could live more economically and make very good money. Almost everyone who lives on Nantucket year-round is here by choice. We chose to live in a place with astronomical rents, milk prices, and summer traffic. If we were really so worried about the bills, we would sell and move to Fitchburg.

We should wise up in September and be a tourist. No one comes to Nantucket for the ice cream, the freshly pressed sheets, or the fine cold beverages. They all come for the beaches, the sailing, the history and the moors. If we could take the black and green blinders off for a week or so, we might be able to see it.

It would be nice to see Cisco crowded with familiar faces. The harbor is wide enough for the mega-yachts and the day sailors. Golf courses and tennis courts can hold all of us now, and the moors would profit from another set of friendly eyes.

If we were to take our vacation on island, perhaps we would start to view Nantucket with the affection that our friend in Hartford has. I doubt if all of the islanders would get misty looking at calendar photos, but perhaps we would think twice about greenlighting more development in Sconset. Perhaps an afternoon of clamming may make some landscapers more hesitant about dumping the fertilizers on the lawn. A few trips to the sandwich shop could help the waitresses see how far a smile will take them. Perhaps buying groceries for a family might help the managers at Stop and Shop.

Nantucket eyes are not that different from Hartford eyes. Everyone is a native somewhere; be it on the mainland or out to sea. We spend so much time mowing the lawn in front of million dollar views, we ignore the million dollar view in our own backyard. Our friend is in Hartford and he knows that it is perfect on Nantucket right now. Maybe we should learn a little something from him.

25: Waiting for the Hurricane

Like many others, I have this deep, abiding love of hurricanes. Sometime in the midst of August, my fancy turns to the Weather Channel and that most passive of all hopes for storm. I watch them form south of the Azores, march westward, and then turn north.

Now, I am sound enough in my mind to understand that a tarantella from the swirling ladies of the Caribbean would do a lot of nasty, personal damage. I don't want to see my roof somersaulting through the wind on it's way to town, nor do I want to live in a house with two boys, but no water or electricity for a week or so. I am sympathetic to the Ratners and their geotubes. If I faced the blank, gray face of roiling nature, I might do the exact same thing. The rational part of my mind that buys broccoli and pays electric bills likes seeing those hurricanes whip out to sea south of us. But the rational part of my mind does not control the remote control.

My love of hurricanes comes from three unpleasant facets of my personality. First, hurricane watching is a passive experience. Hurricanes are the perfect sofa sport; I can do nothing to either bring or deflect "Juan" as he forms over the Gulf Stream. If I practice my chipping often enough, my golf scores will go down. But there is nothing I can do to make "Juan's" cloud tops colder. Second, I like to bear witness and survive. I would like to one day be an old coot at the Hub declaiming "The Big One" to all who will listen.

Finally and most importantly, I want a Hurricane because it will be a big reset button for the island. A category four will come staggering over Madaquecham and flatten the place, forcing us all to start again. "Juan" will wipe it all clean. Multi-million dollar houses will blow away like tinker toys and the architects finest work will wash up at Dionis. Then we can all start fresh.

"Juan," however, will blow out to sea far to our east and that great "reset" will remain out off the coast for the foreseeable future. No storm will ever come and clear

Nantucket back into the fifties or earlier. Meanwhile, the Ratners and the rest of us need to worry about the flood.

The incoming flood of money should have those of us who live on and love the island more than a little worried. In the last three weeks, the island's papers have reported on another private golf course, a huge fund-raiser at the golf club, and one hundred billionaires. A quick walk through the Real Estate Review shows at least twenty properties for sale for over 5 million a piece. Nantucket has moved from Chatham to Woodstock to Aspen while we have been cleaning sand from our toes.

At the same time that the plutocrats Gulfstream in here, the Peeps have their moving sales and are shipping out on the rising tide. Some are leaving rich from a nice sale. Some are leaving poor with cancelled rent checks. But they are all leaving.

The flood that forces them out comes from increased costs and decreased wages. Rent costs more. The boat will cost more. Taxes (for sewer) will cost a lot more. Groceries and gas cost more. Day-care costs more. Doctors and medicine cost more. Meanwhile, building is down and fly-over workers continue to take jobs and projects that would have gone to Nantucket firms in the past. Leslie Goodspeed (who I wish well) is the new Nantucket worker. She comes in on the first flight and leaves on the last.

For a year-round family, $2000 rent (or mortgage) plus $600 in groceries plus $1200 in health insurance plus $800 a month day care adds up to one way to Hyannis. The money no longer comes in to offset this; not from his job, her job, renting the house, or selling the kids. Madaket Sunsets and Sanford Farm Strolls are wonderful things, but they don't bring in the do-re-mi.

The Gulfstreams will keep coming. The Boston Pops will bring more plutocrats eager for south-west winds and sand in their shoes. The island will change again, to an island of waiters, caterers, realtors, golf pros, and landscapers. We will move inexorably to being the Country Club off Cape.

So, when the rest of us move off to the lovely old farmhouse in Colchester, we will put our photos in the albums and mount the pictures in the hall. Books will still have sand in their spines and the summer clothes will hide under the polarfleece. And in August, we will still watch the Weather Channel and wait for the Category Five that will bring us back home.

26: A Lover's Quarrel

Down the street, a maple tree is beginning its turn. The outer leaves, on the eastern side of the tree, have started to catch fire, while the rest of the leaves wait to burn. Otherwise, yellow leaves have started to fall from the elms and they fill in the gutters by the side of the road. I pass by these as I walk to work and, like the perpetual truant, I kick them up into a flurry of color.

It's hard not to love the Berkshires. The crowds, such as they were, have left. The color begins the change at the top of the Adirondacks, and then slowly seeps lower and lower. Pleasant surprises arise around each corner, whether it be the quiet bubble of the Housatonic, the gentle rise of Mount Greylock, or the pine primeval darkness of Monument Mountain. Great Barrington and Lenox hold historic and architectural treasures, as well as remarkable Chinese food, a variety of micro-brews, and golf courses with greens fees less expensive than a downtown cocktail. There is a lot to love.

And yet, I don't.

With an inward eye, I look back on the moors turning russet in Madaket, the view of the ocean from Ram's Pasture, and the sight of the fog bank crossing the first hole at Miacomet. Outside, the Berkshires throws herself at me in a wanton display of color and glory, but my heart keeps crossing that vast Nantucket Sound to my old, dear friend.

I remember when I fell in love with the island. One morning in late September two decades ago, I woke up early to bike to school. Standing outside of the rented house on Meadowview Drive, I stood in the blueblack of early morning. The ducks circled the pond, the Canadian breeze stirred the hedges, but otherwise the air was more still and silent than I had ever heard before. And in that silence, I recognized the distant roll of waves onto the beach.

I think many people fall in love with the island. Some of our summer visitors have her as an exotic and exciting mistress, with extravagant gifts of fish and golf. Other visitors perceive Nantucket as an old lover who was too wild and impractical for a long term, but who holds so many rich memories. Natives may see her as a mother who nurtures but demands. They may only feel her love when they leave.

Those who have chosen to live out here can probably pick a moment when they realized that they had fallen in love with the island. More likely than not, I suspect those moments came as glances or quiet moments of grace rather than the splendor of a Sconset sunrise or the starry whirl of a December night. I remember the love tokens the island has sent me. She sent me pockets of early fog on the Madaket Road, when the car would dip under and above the clouds. She gave us a pheasant to visit our backyard at 4:30 every afternoon and a Snowy Owl to swoop over me out on the cranberry bogs. The island dropped a small fish in a puddle in front of me and watched one with a gentler heart than mine run to drop it off in the ocean. On what proved to be my mother's last visit, she sent a freak snow squall in October to whiten my Mom's clothes while she stood atop Altar Rock. She turned to my father and said "I have to spend another night." And so she did.

Over time, I developed deep, marital love for the island. We have been troubled by the gray swells and heartened by moments of glad grace; our pleasures have become routine but our routines have become pleasures. I no longer stop to listen to the storm waves pound the beach but let it follow me as if it was a song I heard her sing in the morning. I have become accustomed to her public beauty of August, but surprised by her hidden and private splendor in December. I remember her green youth and see it glowing under her browning age.

For many, Nantucket is too demanding a spouse. You must forgive the greed and the development. You must forgive her brushing old friends off and welcoming the flashy on their jets. She demands money and time and energy. You have to change so much, as she changes.

Separation and divorce seem easy. You sell the house, get a new job, have one last party for your January friends and you leave with your bags and a future with a more reasonable and less fickle land. When you think back on the island, you laugh and joke at it all. Regret melts in your drink.

Long love demands the strength of geology. Beneath the art of wind, and the passion of the waves must lie bedrock. Time, tide, snow, and houses pass overhead and leave the substrata fixed and unbroken. Everything else changes. Families change, jobs change, houses and developments are built, trees and scrub grow, but the island, beneath it all, remains the same. And so we age.

Nantucket cannot love me. It existed long before I trudged its sand and it will exist long after I have been ground into that very sand. That which I love I have projected out onto the sandspit of scrub pines and beach grass. The waves are not generous, the wind is not graceful, and the cold winter light bears no gentle touch. They are what they have always been: fundamental, immutable, and inhuman.

Yet, the truth that the heart knows is that I may still love.

Nearby, Robert Frost is buried in a simple grave in the Old Bennington Cemetery. A hero in a tragic life, he buried most of his children, and his beloved wife, Elinor. Under her name, Frost put his tenderest view of marriage; "wing to wing and oar to oar." Under his name is written "I had a lover's quarrel with the world." The old widower loved a world that would never love him back. The woods of New Hampshire and Vermont would never work oar to oar with him as Elinor had. Yet he still loved, and quarreled, with those hills.

I hope I bear the same love for the island. I know I can quarrel with her. The prices, the real estate, the development, the greed, and the blind self-destruction of hedges and houses feed my fighting fire. But at the end of the day, I will still stand underneath her stars and hear the low roll of waves off to the south. I have sand in my shoes. Long may it stay.

27: The Spiderweb That Connects Us

The summer leaves Nantucket as a lover would. He lingers and makes two or three brief forays at breaking up during September, then he tries to work things out during October. Finally, he gets in a fight during Halloween, and moves out sometime deep in November. Sometime after the Vineyard game, the island takes a long bath, puts on sweat pants, watches old movies, and eats pint after pint of Ben and Jerry's.

To know Nantucket in the winter is to know her alone. The people, the stores, the colors, the flowers, and the leaves have long since walked away and left her. And that's okay. Without the beauty of bloom and color, the island reveals handsome vistas and open sky. Huge clouds of birds pass off the south shore, implacable gray waves thunder along the beach without even the dream of surfers, and the winter sunlight glows gold on the sand and brush.

Winter has little patience with foolishness and illusion. The island lies naked on the water; all of the practical and lucrative images of summer have dropped to the ground. Gray waves continually roll in from the horizon The empty sky opens up through the dark fingers of trees. There are no flowers, no leaves, no charming green grass or great deep blue ocean. Beneath the cunning paints of summer, the island is as it always was; brown, wet, and sandy. The wind does not blow for golf balls or sailboats, the waves do not curl for surfers to ride, and the sky does not glow for the painters and photographers. Nantucket is cold, handsome, and indifferent in the winter.

Our summer visitors never get this. When they stand at the beach in Shimmo in July, the land and the water blaze with light and sound. In November, the only human sound comes from the church bells across the harbor.

In the winter, you are left with your thoughts and your pulse. Sooner or later, you walk a street or a path in the moors and find yourself. There you are; cold, alone, and standing on a sandy trail amid the bare ruined choirs of scrub oak and elm. You can't get cocky about your latest memo or your latest sale while you stand in front the eternal onslaught of waves.

I met winter on the boat last night. I stood alone on deck and watched the winter sun set over Nantucket Sound. Bright and clear, the sun dropped behind one line of cloud before it moved inexorably beneath the horizon. The last sprinting low clouds caught the final golden light and glowed. Remarkably ordinary, I witnessed it alone on the boat.

I was alone for the previous sunset as well. I had been waiting at a light on Route 44 in Connecticut behind ten other cars and ten drivers. The sun set between Staples and Petsmart, with NPR on the radio and a destination in mind. Off-island, it's easy to get blinded by routes and deafened by noise. Just because the radio says that you are a valued listener doesn't make it so.

The central irony of winter living is that while you are alone in nature, you aren't alone. During these winter months, Nantucketers reaffirm the spiderweb of tradition, consideration, and fibs that connect us to one another. Without all of the summer visitors cluttering up the stores and the streets, we can finally see each other eye to eye, whether we want to or not. Nantucket, in the winter, becomes the ultimate New England small town.

Forgiveness and humor are more important in the winter than heating oil and DVDs. We are all naked. The neighbor's misfortune that amuses you today could be your own tomorrow. The sin that you can't countenance this week is spread across your face next week. So you wave and smile.

On that same boat trip, long after the sunset, I walked down to my car. Midway up the platform, a knock startled me. I looked up and a former student was waving. Two cars up, it was a former co-worker. A little further along, someone I only vaguely remember. But they waved and smiled and I waved back. Each wave reaffirms the spiderweb that connects us.

Unfortunately, that spiderweb is burning. As costs and prices rise, young families leave the island for the land of Home Depot and Costco. The logic of living on a lottery ticket escapes them. Meanwhile, many of the high paying jobs fly over with full lunch buckets in the morning and fly back with empty ones in the evening. Our leaders turn the calendars back to 1997 and can't imagine why there isn't another ten years of building boom left. Then they look to the fifth grade to pay for it. When the island sells one billion dollars in real estate by October, more of it should stay here. Yet the money slips away faster than the sand. Nantucket loses community as it becomes a commodity: the pig does not profit by the trade in pork bellies.

Selling Nantucket as a commodity means selling it as an illusion. A realtor comes to an empty spot on the moors, erects a two-story platform, and asks his clients to imagine a house there. "Sure, the land looks ugly naked, but imagine a nice 10,000 square foot neo-colonial. And we can cover up that unsightly bulge with a putting green." The clients go downtown and see themselves as caught up in the same spiderweb of island community that their money burns away. Perhaps it will be replaced by another web of clubs and tennis matches or perhaps not.

In the end, the island will still exist, whether there will be community or not. The visitors come, the visitors go, but the earth abideth forever. The enduring, abiding truth of winter is that we have no more permanence out here than snowmen. The sun will set, the wind will blow, and the waves will break long after the putting green has grown out and the viewing stand has fallen. Winter on Nantucket is living without illusions. And loving it.

28: The Moment of the Race Car Tent

On Nantucket, the holiday season begins with the Vineyard game. Sometime during the game, the great gray lid of winter fastens itself over the island, the wind picks up, a few flakes hit your cheeks, and its time to find the wool and seal the windows. The only tourists on island are rooting for those fellows in purple. The stands and fences are jammed with familiar faces blowing on familiar hands and stomping familiar feet in the cold. Looks like it is just us again, doesn't it?

The Vineyard game is a checkpoint for dozens of men in the stands. Their memory still holds the feel of the open field tackle, the fumbled handoff, and the leaping catch in the end zone. Every one of those men, in the dark corner of their minds, thinks that if they had a month to get back in shape, they could still play the game.

I would think it pathetic if I didn't believe it myself. My memory has been more faithful than my muscles. I remember the locker, the plays, the pads, and the walk up to

Landrigan Field. I was an indifferent player on a bad team; I cared about far more things that Saturday's results. But if I could play again, I would be a Johnny Damon level "idiot" and just enjoy throwing myself around.

My fellow football fantasists and I stand behind the fence with our hands in our pockets watching the game. I don't think we want any more football glory; I think we realize that we didn't enjoy it then as much as we could have. All of the slings and arrows of adolesence were upon us and prevented us from enjoying the pleasure of whacking each other. Were I to pick up the phone and call my younger self, I would tell him to stop worrying about the future and start enjoying the present. Get in there and hit somebody.

Perhaps my octogenarian self will put down his beer, call me up and tell me the same thing. Stop worrying and enjoy the days. Don't worry about national politics, the career, the sewers and the missed putts. Enjoy every sandwich.

The holiday season is a good time to think of that octogenarian in the future. When I come to the checkpoints of the holidays, I usually think of what is lost. Culling out and editing a greeting card list is one of the ugliest jobs of the season. This one divorced, this one married, this one's address is gone, this one has a new child, and this one passed away. My future self would counsel me to focus on those names that remain. Holidays should be a good time to celebrate what abides and endures, not bewailing what is gone forever.

This may be a good thought to have as Christmas Stroll looms on the calendar. For many islanders, Stroll is always a good time to remember how it used to be; there were less people, more bargains, and better snacks. Now, the town will be sick with credit cards in mink, with flashing earrings and musical ties. They come in force, take over those inns and restaurants that remain, then leave their money with Santa. For islanders, going home and hiding under the soft ooze from the TV seems very attractive.

But if Christmas Stroll were just the waltz of the wallets, it would never have abided and endured. Cobblestones and Christmas trees can be found closer to New York at a fraction of the cost. No one gets seasick or has to sit outside on the New York Thruway.

However, the strollers do not really come to shop. They come to sink into the atmosphere for a weekend. They want to walk around, eat chowder, meet friends, have cocktails, and buy pants with embroidered trees. They like the children's holiday decorations, the carolers, the town crier, and the funny hats. To them it feels like Christmas. When we go home and work on our TV tans, does it feel like Christmas? If my 80-year-old, beer-drinking self called me up, would he recommend that I keep turning channels until I found another "Law and Order"? Or would he want me downtown in funny hat next to the tree with the most toy trucks on it?

Time robs us of everything, anyway. Time took away the pleasure of football as it will, eventually, take away the pleasure of friends and family. When we only think of what we want or will lose, we miss what we have. Then, the clock runs out, everyone shakes hands, and you turn in your helmet and shoulder pads forever. While we can, we should sit on a bench and watch the funny clothes and hats go by. Since we can't make time stand still, perhaps we can tickle it.

Two years ago, my oldest boy figured out that Christmas meant presents. When he came downstairs, he found a Formula One race car that doubled as tent. For twenty minutes, he missed every other present that was waiting for him under the tree. Instead, he crawled under that tent, made racing car sounds, and crawled around the living room. The other presents could wait; they would eventually get their turn and his undivided attention. This, however, was the moment for the race car tent.

My Christmas wish for my son is that he forgets the race car tent. Rather, when he sees that first present under the tree, he immerses himself in it and loves the moment as it happens, without second thoughts, memories, or regrets. Enjoy the now. Life is too short to stand behind the team bench waiting for the past to call your number and send you in.